Exam Practice
A LEVEL

D1556358

A Level
Exam Practice

Covers AS and A2

History

Author

Russell Williams

Contents

AS and A2 exams

Different types of questions

We have used two types of questions in this exam practice book: structured questions and extended essays.

Structured questions

Almost all of the questions in AS History examination papers are structured questions. These are sub-divided to test your understanding and knowledge of different parts of the topic. They usually become progressively more difficult.

Extended essays

Almost all of the questions in A2 History examination questions are extended essays. They test more detailed knowledge and understanding and require more varied arguments than structured questions.

What examiners look for

- Answers should contain sound knowledge, good understanding and accurate discussions. Examiners do not expect AS answers to contain detailed knowledge but you must show that you can use knowledge accurately and relevantly.

- Answers must be relevant. Focus on the question and discuss the key issues.

- Make sure that your answers are organised. Discuss the major issues first, then less important factors.

- Write accurately. Spelling, punctuation and a clear style are important.

What makes an A, C and E grade candidate?

Obviously, you want to get the highest grade that you can. The way to do this is to show that you have a sound understanding and knowledge of the topics that you have studied and can express yourself clearly.

- **A grade candidates** always write relevantly. They use their knowledge to explain and analyse. Answers are accurately written. The minimum mark for an A grade candidate is 80%.

- **C grade candidates** write answers that are relevant but often include description or narrative instead of analysis and explanation. Answers are mostly accurately written. The minimum mark for a C grade candidate is 60%.

- **E grade candidates** have a basic knowledge and understanding and, sometimes contain unnecessary material. Answers contain a number of writing errors. The minimum mark for an E grade candidate is 40%.

Successful revision

Revision skills

- Draw up a revision timetable to cover all the aspects of the examination in plenty of time. Give yourself deadlines to complete stages of revision.

- Revise regularly. Do not concentrate too long on one module but balance your revision.

- Regular revision works better than last-minute and late-night work.

- Highlight your notes with a marker-pen but do not make your notes unintelligible by too many additions.

- Concentrate on understanding, not memorising. You will remember if you understand. You will not necessarily understand if you only memorise.

- Think about the possible questions that you might be asked and those you have done during your course.

- Plan and write practice answers and this will help you to improve and be write longer answers.

- Stop before you get too tired.

- Switch off when you are not revising!

Practice questions

This book is designed to help you to get better results.

- Look at the grade A and C candidates' answers. Why are the A answers better?

- Try the exam practice questions and then evaluate your responses by looking at the answers.

- Make sure that you understand why the answers given are correct.

- When you are ready, try the AS and A2 mock exam questions.

You should do well in the examination if you write good answers to the questions in this book. Remember that success in examinations follows steady and continuous work, not sudden efforts.

Planning and timing your answers in the exams

- Be confident! You have not seen the examination questions previously but you have learned the necessary material and have probably answered similar questions in revision.

- The question paper will tell you how many marks are awarded to each part and this will be a guide to the time that you should spend on each part.

- Read the questions carefully. There are no hidden traps.

- Write only the number of the question. Do not write out the question.

- Write a very brief plan. Plans are not marked but they help you to organise your answer.

- Write first about the most important aspects of the topic, then the less important.

- Leave a little time at the end of the examination to check your answers.

How to boost your grade

- Do not write abbreviations *(gov* for government / *Bis* for Bismarck*)*. Avoid notes unless in an emergency.

- Concentrate on explanation and analysis. Avoid narrative that only tells a story.

- Every question has a key instruction such as 'Explain', 'Why', 'Examine the view that'. Pay attention to these key instructions in your answer. They are usually the first words in a question. Underline the key issue and the key words in a question to help you to concentrate on them.

- Answer all parts of the question and pay attention to dates in the question.

- Do not write long introductions or describe the background. Discuss the question itself as soon as possible. A good introduction can show what you think is most important.

- Do not write conclusions that only repeat what you have said already. Conclusions should emphasise the main points.

- The length of the sources in some examinations varies and your teacher will advise you about the time you should spend reading the sources, usually about 20% of the total time for the examination. Read the sources first very quickly to get an idea of what they are about, then more slowly for the details. Underline important parts of the sources. There will be useful clues in the title. Often, each source has a short introduction. There is always an attribution or identification of the writer, with a date. These will help you to understand the sources.

- Do not write paraphrases or summaries of the sources. References can be written quickly *(line 3* or in a brief quotation, *'Hitler was... appeasement by Britain'.)* Does the question ask you to use only the sources or the sources and your own knowledge?

- Practise writing accurately before the examination. Examiners know that examination pressures lead to careless mistakes but you must get in the habit of correct spelling, punctuation and organisation. Write legibly. Marks are not given for handwriting but make it easy for the examiner to understand your writing.

Key issues, examiner's tips and examiner's commentary

- The answers to the Exam practice questions and Mock Examinations contain 'Key Issues' and 'Examiner's tips' about every question. Read ALL of these and make use of them in your revision and in the examinations.

- 'Key Issues' focus your attention on the most important part of the question 'Examiner's tips' tell you how best to organise your answer. For example, 'Compare the importance of three factors in the downfall of Napoleon III.' The **Key Issue** is the comparison of three reasons for the fall of the Second Empire. Therefore ignore the rise of Napoleon III. Do not tell the story of the Second Empire. **Examiner's tips** are 'Comparison should be organised, showing similarities and differences. Consider reasons in order of importance. Focus on 1870 – 71, relating earlier developments to these years.'

- Write down the Key Issues when you plan your answer and put them in order. Write about the most important issues first.

- 'Examiner's tips' often tell you to be relevant and avoid narrative. Analysis gets higher marks than description. Follow this advice when you write your answers.

Questions with model answers

C grade candidate – mark scored 6/10

For help: See Revise AS Modern British and European History Study Guide pages 40–45

To what extent was British foreign policy consistent between 1815 and 1865?

[WJEC question]

Examiner's Commentary

The most important statesmen involved in British foreign policy during this period were Castlereagh, Canning and Palmerston ✔.

> No major gaps in leading statesmen.

Castlereagh was at the Congress of Vienna (1815) and defended Britain's interests by gaining important naval bases. He also helped to build a balance of power between the most important European countries, Britain, Austria, Prussia and Russia. He supported regular meetings or congresses of these major countries and favoured France's admittance to the Congress System at Aix-la-Chapelle in 1818. However, he opposed the Holy Alliance which was suggested by Alexander I of Russia to guarantee absolute monarchs and frontiers and crush revolutions because it might lead to intervention in other countries' affairs. He became increasingly unhappy with the policies of the congresses and was suspicious of Austrian and Russian motives. He took little part in the Congress of Laibach in 1821 ✗.

> Too much narrative in this paragraph.

After Castlereagh died in 1822, Canning agreed with many of his policies, especially non-intervention in other countries. He opposed action against the liberals in Spain and recognised the independence of Spanish colonies on South America. Like Castlereagh, he was suspicious of the Congress System He also wished to encourage British trade. The Greek revolt caused problems for Canning because many people supported Greek independence but Canning was suspicious of Russia, which was an ally of Greece against the Ottoman Empire. In the end, Canning co-operated with Russia to help Greece become independent, sinking an Ottoman fleet at Navarino in 1827.

Palmerston was in charge of foreign affairs for most of the period from 1830 to 1865 ✗.

> The answer is sequential: it deals first with Castlereagh, then Canning and finally Palmerston. A better answer would have focused on the similarities and differences between Castlereagh, Canning and Palmerston. The answer only discusses the key issue of consistency indirectly.

His most important aim was to defend the interests of Britain as a great country and he was willing to use force to achieve these aims. Although it involved Britain in quarrels with other countries, he was usually popular in Britain. In Europe, he opposed French influence in Belgium. He also opposed French ambitions in Spain and Portugal in the 1830s. In the Eastern Question, Palmerston, like Canning, was suspicious of Russia and he tried to make sure that the Ottoman Empire did not become weaker. He would intervene wherever British interests were involved, for example in the Opium War in China and in the Don Pacifico Affair. In his later years, Palmerston negotiated the end of the Crimean War and supported Cavour in bringing

Questions with model answers

C grade candidate continued

 For help: See Revise AS Modern British and European History Study Guide pages 40–45

Examiner's Commentary

about Italian unification. He also had a number of failures, for example in the Chinese Wars (1856-60) and by his policy on the American Civil War. He was unsuccessful in opposing Bismarck's schemes to increase the power of Prussia ✔.

> An understanding and knowledge of the period as a whole from 1815 to 1865. Answer is always relevant.

A grade candidate – mark scored 8/10

*Explain **briefly** the main aims of British foreign policy in 1815.*

[WJEC question]

The most important aim of foreign policy in 1815 was to achieve a lasting peace after the Napoleonic wars. These wars had been a major threat to Britain's security and had been very expensive to wage ✔.

> Concentrates on explanation not narrative.

Castlereagh, the Foreign Secretary, did not want to humiliate France because it might seek revenge in the future but thought that it was necessary to create buffer states to prevent more French aggression. It was also important to have a balance of power between the major European countries so that Austria, Prussia or Russia would not become too strong. With France weakened, it was possible that one or more of these countries would try to dominate Europe ✔.

> Well organised, explaining a variety of aims, and includes enough knowledge to prove the points.

These countries gained European territories and influence in the Vienna settlement but Britain was more interested in keeping its naval supremacy because its economy was increasingly dependent on international trade. In the settlement, Britain gained the naval bases of Heligoland, Malta, Mauritius, Trinidad, Tobago, St. Lucia and the Cape of Good Hope ✔.

> Answer is brief, very relevant and clearly written.

Exam practice questions

Answers on p. 10

Source-based question: The 1832 Reform Act

(1) **Source 1** *T. B. Macaulay, speech in the House of Commons on parliamentary reform, 2 March 1831.*

Unless this measure, or some similar measure, be speedily adopted, great and terrible calamities will befall us. I support this measure as a measure of reform; but I support it still more as a measure of conservation. We say, and we say justly, that it is not by mere numbers, but by those with property and education that the nation ought to be governed. Yet we are excluding from all share in government vast numbers of property owners and also many who have good education.

(a) Study Source 1. What, according to Source 1, is Macaulay's attitude to parliamentary reform?

(b) What arguments did those who opposed parliamentary reform use against it in the years 1830–32?

(c) What impact did the Reform Act of 1832 have on the political system in the period to 1850?

[Edexcel question]

(2) **(a)** Explain the problems that Ireland caused for Tory governments from 1829 to 1846.

(b) Assess Peel's success as Prime Minister.

[OCR question]

Answers

(1)   **Key issue: Using a primary source to explain the 1832 Reform Act.**

Focus on the source in (a) and (b). Avoid paraphrase of the source. Use your own knowledge in (c) to give a brief answer.

(a) •   Macaulay supported reform. Necessary to avoid unrest.
     •   Old system did not include many important people who owned property or who were well educated.
     •   He wished to conserve much of the old system ('a measure of conservation').

(b) •   Most Tories and some Whigs believed that democracy was dangerous. It would cause disorder. They remembered the effects of the French Revolution.
     •   Landowners and wealthy businessmen would be more responsible than the new electorate when voting. System of small and 'rotten' boroughs was traditional. Abolishing them would destroy private rights.
     •   Some people agreed with minor changes but thought that the existing system worked well and had made Britain great. Fears that the industrial centres would gain power from the agricultural and landed areas.
     •   The Act might be the first step to other reforms, perhaps leading to the abolition of the House of Lords and the monarchy.
     •   Some believed that the proposals did not go far enough. Would not benefit all of the working classes. Riots in London, Bristol, Derby and Nottingham, as well as in some country districts.

(c) •   1832 Reform Act had important effects on the political system. More than 200,000 new voters but not always clear who had the right to vote. Few members of the working class had the franchise.
     •   Some supporters of reform disappointed by the Act. Most of the parliamentary seats were still in the south of England. Most MPs were landowners and many were aristocrats. Bribery and corruption continued in the voting system, not least because of the lack of a secret ballot. Most attempts to get rid of the corruption failed.
     •   Reform Act encouraged other reforms. Whigs, supported by the radicals, introduced changes, for example the Factory Acts in the 1830s and 1840s, the Poor Law Amendment Act and Municipal Corporations Act. Many of these did little to improve the lives of the working classes. The new Poor Law system was very unpopular.
     •   Chartism developed in the 1840s partly because of disappointment with the 1832 Reform Act. The Charter demanded major political changes.

(2)   **Key issue: Explanation of the Tory governments and the Irish problem.**

Focus on the period 1829–46 mentioned in the question. Avoid general discussions of the Irish problem. Link to the Tory governments.

(a) •   Overall: Ireland continued to be one of the most serious problems faced by Tory governments. 1 – Roman Catholic Emancipation, 2 – land, 3 – the Irish Famine.

- Religion: The Tories, supported by George IV, believed strongly in the Church of England. Unwilling to allow Catholics to vote or to become MPs. Large majority of the Irish were Roman Catholic, excluded from the vote and Parliament.
- Emancipation: Pressure for change increased during the 1820s. O'Connell founded the Catholic Association to fight for emancipation and the repeal of the Union. Violence in Ireland and civil war threatened. O'Connell won an election. Could not take his seat in Parliament because of his religion.
- Tory divisions: Peel, the Home Secretary and previously Chief Secretary for Ireland, supported emancipation. Wellington, the Prime Minister, accepted it unwillingly. Hard-line Tories refused and regarded Peel as a traitor. Division helped the Whigs to come to power.
- Land: Absentee English landlords owned much Irish land. Tenants often lived near starvation. Little security of tenure and no compensation if they were turned out of their homes. Increase in population caused a shortage of land. This caused another division between Peel, sympathetic to the Irish tenants, and other Tories who thought that the rights of the landowners were more important.
- Famine: Famine in the 1840s caused problems for the Tories because they disagreed about the solution. Failure of the potato harvests in 1845 and 1846 resulted in widespread deaths and emigration. Tories who represented farmers and landlords did not wish to interfere with the Corn Laws, which prevented the import of cheap food.
- Peel's attitude: Peel wished to import corn and repeal the Corn Laws. Peel succeeded in introducing repeal. The Tories split again and lost power to the Whigs.

(b)   Key issue: Assessment of Peel as Prime Minister.

Examiner's tip

Assessment involves discussion of achievements and failures. Make clear what you think was more important. Avoid narrative of Peel's career.

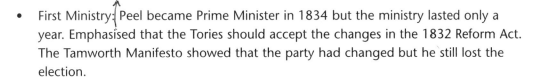

- First Ministry: Peel became Prime Minister in 1834 but the ministry lasted only a year. Emphasised that the Tories should accept the changes in the 1832 Reform Act. The Tamworth Manifesto showed that the party had changed but he still lost the election.
- Second Ministry: His most important ministry was from 1841 to 1846. Peel favoured free trade. Budgets improved industry and reduced the cost of living. Income tax was reintroduced. Social reforms included a Mines Act and a Factory Act. He was defeated because of the crisis in Ireland. Many members of the Tory Party would not accept the end of protectionism even if it was the solution to the famine in Ireland.
- Peel's personality: Cold man personally with a quick temper. Admired for his cleverness. Peel did not completely unite the Tories. Rivalry between him and Disraeli. Many Tories preferred the interests of agriculture to those of trade and industry which Peel encouraged.
- Overall judgement: Peel persuaded his party to accept the 1832 Reform Act. Helped the Tories to win power. Many attempts to introduce reforms, especially in economic policy. Preferred to split his party over the Irish Famine because he was in favour of free trade and against many Tories who were protectionist.

Questions with model answers

C grade candidate – mark scored 6/10

For help: See Revise AS Modern British and European History Study Guide pages 31–33

Assess Gladstone's success as Prime Minister from 1868 to 1874.

Examiner's Commentary

Gladstone's first ministry from 1868 to 1874 introduced some very important reforms ✔.

→ Relevant answer which deals with a range of issues.

In 1870, Forster's Education Act established elementary schools although attendance was not compulsory. The civil service was reformed and examinations were introduced. In 1871, the University Test acts allowed Protestant nonconformists to teach at the universities of Oxford and Cambridge. An act recognised trades unions although the Criminal Law Amendment act made picketing illegal so that it was difficult to organise strikes ✗.

→ This paragraph is very descriptive. The answer needs more assessment of the key issue, Gladstone's success.

The Ballot Act of 1872 introduced secret ballots in elections as the Chartists had demanded. The Licensing Act tried to deal with the problem of drunkenness by giving magistrates the power to license pubs and limit opening times. Cardwell's army reforms improved the selection and training of officers and made a career in the army more attractive by abolishing extreme punishments and reducing the length of service.

Gladstone's main aim was to `pacify Ireland' ✗.

→ Poor organisation. Ireland was the main aim and therefore should have been examined first.

After separating the Irish Church from the state his government passed the Irish Land act, which benefited poor tenants and peasants. However, this did not solve the Irish problem. Gladstone's foreign policy also seemed weak when Britain did not intervene in the Franco-Prussian War and had to pay compensation to the USA for damage to shipping during the American Civil War. By 1874, Gladstone had lost the support of many voters and lost the election ✔.

→ Answer gets credit for accurate historical knowledge.

A grade candidate – mark scored 8/10

For help: See Revise AS Modern British and European History Study Guide pages 31–33

Why did the Liberals gain power in 1868?

Examiner's Commentary

Although Disraeli and the Tories introduced the Reform Act of 1867 that doubled the size of the electorate and benefited urban working class men, the Liberals under Gladstone won the election of 1868. Gladstone was a very effective speaker in the election campaign, travelling widely to address large crowds and the Liberals also had other able leaders such as Bright and Forster. Disraeli conducted a more traditional election campaign that had less appeal. The new voters believed that the Liberals had been more enthusiastic about electoral reform although the Conservatives introduced it. Disraeli had largely introduced the bill as `a leap in the dark´ without being completely committed to change ✔.

Focused on the key issue of 1868. The background is linked to this.

Major issues in the campaign favoured the Liberals. Gladstone was determined to solve the Irish problem especially by freeing the Irish Church from its links with the state. The Conservatives´ opposition to this proposal was unpopular with many of the nonconformist middle class and other townspeople who were not supporters of the Church.

Both Gladstone and Disraeli became leaders of their parties just before the 1868 election but had been important throughout the 1860s. Another similarity was that they had both been Chancellor of the Exchequer. Gladstone had gained a high reputation as a defender of free trade and low taxes. It was clear that he would be the future leader of the party and he dominated the Liberals after the death of Palmerston in 1865 ✔.

Well organised. The answer explains short-term issues then longer-term factors.

Disraeli´s control of the Conservatives was less certain. He had been partly responsible for the split in the Conservatives over the Corn Laws that had defeated Peel in 1846 and, although clever, was not fully trusted by his colleagues. His Jewish background was also a disadvantage. He had changed his policies several times, for example from protectionism to free trade, and many suspected that the introduction of the Reform Act was another unscrupulous device to gain power ✔.

A balanced answer. Explains how Conservatives' weaknesses contributed to Liberals' success.

The result was that the Liberals, not the Conservatives, benefited from the Reform Act and gained a large majority. However, Disraeli and the Conservatives were to gain in the long term because distrust had disappeared at the time of the next election in 1874, which Disraeli won ✔.

The brief conclusion puts 1868 into a wider context.

Exam practice questions

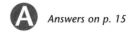

Answers on p. 15

(1)   Source-based question: The Poor Law

Source 1 *From* A Political History 1868–1900, *by R.A. Cross, 1903.*

Taking it as a starting point that, apart from the proper administration of the Poor Law, it is not the duty of the state to provide any class of citizens with any of the necessities of life … but, at the same time, it is the right and duty of the state to interfere in sanitary laws … I brought in and carried a Bill to enable local authorities to buy up the old rookeries [urban slum areas] and rebuild … Although much remains still to be done, all the really large old rookeries in London were swept away under this Act.

What, according to Source 1, is Cross's attitude towards the role of the State in social legislation?

[Edexcel question]

(2)   Source-based question: Irish Home Rule

Source 2 *Lord Randolph Churchill, a leading Conservative, addresses a meeting in Ulster about Home Rule, in Union Hall, Belfast, 22 February 1886.*

If political parties and political leaders should be so utterly lost to every feeling and dictate of honour and courage as to hand over coldly, and for the sake of purchasing a short period of parliamentary peace, the lives and liberties of the Loyalists of Ireland to their hereditary and most bitter foes – Ulster will not be a consenting party. Ulster will fight, Ulster will be right.

(a)   Study Source 2. From this source and your own knowledge, explain why Ulster was such an important consideration in the Home Rule question in 1886.

Source 3 *Cardinal Cullen, an Irish Cardinal, expresses his concerns about Home Rule in the Catholic journal* The Tablet, *27 March 1886.*

I do not like this new movement for Home Rule because I am convinced that the first future attack on the liberty of the Irish church and religion will come from a native Irish parliament. I am convinced that the moving spirit in this new Home Rule movement is nothing but Revolutionary. A revolutionary Irish parliament would pass laws that are subversive of justice, morality and religion, just as has been done in Italy since unification. I, for one, can never advocate such a revolutionary movement.

(b)   Study Source 3. How reliable is Source 3 in explaining opposition in Ireland to Home Rule?

[OCR question]

(3)   Examine the principles that guided British foreign policy during the period 1868–1902.

Answers

(1) **Key issue: Using a primary source to explain support for the new Poor Law.**

- Cross believed that state, that is government, intervention in people's lives should be limited.
- The State should take action to prevent extreme poverty. This was generally accepted at the time.
- Cross was willing to go further. The State should also prevent unsanitary conditions by introducing laws against poor housing. Local authorities were given the power to take over slum areas.

(2) (a) **Key issue: Explanation of the importance of Ulster in Irish Home Rule.**

- Conservatives and many Liberals opposed the first Home Rule Bill in 1886. Lord Randolph Churchill, a leading Conservative, was one of the most extreme critics.
- Source 2 emphasises the importance of Ulster. Churchill was willing even to encourage a rebellion by the Ulstermen. 'Ulster will fight, Ulster will be right.' Claimed that Gladstone's policies were a danger to 'the lives and liberties of the Loyalists'. Would cause violence in Ireland and in England.
- Most Irishmen were Roman Catholic but the population of Ulster was mostly Protestant. Called Loyalists because they opposed any moves towards self-government or independence.
- Speech was a turning point because the fate of Ulster became more important in the argument about Irish Home Rule. Churchill played an important part in forming a Unionist party against Gladstone. Home Rule Bill was defeated. Ulster continued to be a divisive issue in attempts to solve the Irish problem.

(b) **Key issue: Assessment of the reliability of a source.**

- Source 3: Not all Roman Catholics were in favour of Irish Home Rule. Cardinal Cullen was an important religious figure. Views were expressed in an official Catholic journal, *The Tablet*. Source is reliable about Cullen's opinions, expressing clearly his fears of revolution in Ireland.
- Most Irish Roman Catholics supported Home Rule. Nationalists won many seats in Irish constituencies in the 1885 general election. This weakens source's reliability.

Answers

- Previous attempts by Gladstone and the Liberals to deal with Ireland by introducing land reform and freeing the Church failed to satisfy the Irish. Repressive measures, including the imprisonment of Parnell, increased the violence that Cullen feared. Most Irish Protestants opposed Home Rule but Cullen shows that some Roman Catholics opposed the violence that could follow Home Rule. Therefore the source is only partly reliable as an expression of Irish opinion.

(3)   **Key issue: Examination of the principles of British foreign policy, 1868–1902.**

Examiner's tip

Pay attention to the dates in the question. Explanation of principles is more important than narrative.

- Gladstone's priorities were in Britain and Ireland. Foreign affairs were very important to other politicians such as Salisbury. For much of the time, Britain was not involved in the European alliances ('splendid isolation'). 'Splendid isolation' was coming to an end by 1902, although Britain was not fully involved in European diplomacy.
- Trade continued to be important. Politicians took more active interest in developing the British Empire, which sometimes resulted in rivalries with continental countries. Some, such as Disraeli, were enthusiastic supporters of imperial expansion. Others, such as Gladstone, did so more reluctantly.
- Fear of Russian ambitions began earlier in the nineteenth century. Britain's interests in the Mediterranean and India. This began to change. Growing opposition to the way in which Turkey governed the Christian peoples of the Balkans. Britain was not a firm ally of Russia by 1902 but the earlier suspicion had weakened. For much of the nineteenth century, Britain had been friendly towards Prussia and then Germany. By 1902 Germany was a growing threat to British interests and Britain became closer to France.

Questions with model answers

C grade candidate – mark scored 6/10

 For help: See Revise AS Modern British and European History Study Guide pages 60–61

Why did Britain and its allies not gain a quick victory in the First World War?

Examiner's Commentary

All of the countries which fought in the First World War expected it to end quickly - it would be over by Christmas. The last European wars, fought under Bismarck, had been over in a few weeks. Britain had a small army which was not equipped to fight a long war whilst Germany's Schlieffen Plan was based on a quick war in the west before defeating Russia ✔.

Good introduction, showing expectations in 1914.

The stalemate developed when the British and French armies halted the Schlieffen Plan and both sides used trench warfare. The trenches stretched for hundreds of miles and millions of men died attempting to win slight gains. The most important battles were the Marne, Ypres, the Somme, Verdun and Passchendaele. New weapons were introduced such as gas, tanks and aircraft but could not defeat the Germans in their trenches ✗.

Why did trench warfare prevent a quick victory? Explain your answer.

In the end, Germany was defeated because its enemies were better organised. Foch became the Commander-in-Chief of the allied armies and used more skilful strategy to weaken the German war effort. The British navy mostly controlled the sea and German U-boats failed to prevent food and military supplies reaching Britain. America joined the war after its ships were sunk by Germany's unrestricted submarine warfare and when Germany's plans to help Mexico to win back American territories were published. Fresh American soldiers were crucial to the allied victory. The German lines began to break up and there was unrest at home, resulting in the fall of the government and the abdication of Kaiser William II. Immediately afterwards, Germany agreed to sign a peace ✔.

Clear explanation of the end of the war.

Other reasons for the length of the war was that Germany was also fighting against Russia and could not concentrate on the western front. Although Russia was defeated in 1917 it was too late to win the war against Britain and France. Its allies were unreliable and Italy changed sides ✗.

Why did other allied strategies fail, for example Gallipoli?

A grade candidate – mark scored 8/10

Read the following source and then answer the questions which follow.

From Britain and the Two World Wars, *by Jocelyn Hunt and Sheila Watson, 1990.*

> … from 1916 onwards, Britain first experienced mass conscription for the first time in its history, and put its first mass army into the field. With these perspectives it is interesting to consider … the status and role of women.

Questions with model answers

A grade candidate continued

 For help: See Revise AS Modern British and European History Study Guide pages 57–61

> For whatever reason, increasing numbers of women went to work in munitions factories. In November 1916, for example, 100 women worked at Woolwich Arsenal in London; a year later 30,000 women were employed there.
>
> [AQA question]

Examiner's Commentary

(a) *How would you account for the increase in number of women workers at Woolwich Arsenal between November 1916 and November 1917?*

Conscription was introduced early in 1916 and created gaps in employment. Losses in the trenches and other threats to Britain, such as German submarines, made it necessary to increase the production of munitions if the war effort was to continue. Women had to fill the gaps when more men were recruited ✔.

Answer uses the source and other knowledge to focus on the specified period.

(b) *In what ways did the experiences of the First World War change employment opportunities for women?*

Working in munitions factories was only one of the ways in which women sought new employment. They were in the police force and other public services, for example working on buses and trams. Some drove lorries. Middle class women who were educated worked in banks or as clerks and typists. All these had been male occupations. Traditional female occupations, especially domestic service, declined ✔.

Variety of female occupations is explained.

(c) *How extensively had the status and role of women in society and politics changed by the end of the First World War?*

In the short term, the First World War changed women´s social status considerably. For the first time, they played a major part in the war effort. Wider employment gave them independence and higher pay. As mothers, they were responsible for keeping families going when the men were fighting. Food shortages, the bombing of some areas and the heavy casualties put a heavy burden on the women. However, many of these changes did not continue after the end of the war. Returning soldiers claimed their traditional jobs especially as industrial workers. The most important difference for working class women was that fewer became domestic servants. However, middle class women continued to work as clerks and typists. The proportion who worked was much higher than before the war ✔.

Reference to extent and limits of social change.

In politics, the First World War was vital to the achievement of women´s suffrage. The Suffragettes ended their campaign, which had often been violent, in 1914 and called for women to play a full part in the war effort. Women over 30 were given the vote in 1918, a recognition of their important contribution to winning the war. They were not equal to men who voted at 21 but it was an important political achievement for women ✔.

Brief but clear explanation of political change.

Exam practice question

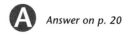

Answer on p. 20

(1) Source-based question: British society between the wars 1919–39

Study the source below and then answer questions **(a)** to **(c)** which follow.

From the recollections of Margaret Cole, a supporter of the General Strike.

The trade unions surrendered, ingloriously, but with ranks unbroken; and though the immediate outcome was, naturally, a falling-off of membership, and a good deal of angry recrimination, the absence of any real revenge, any sacking of the leaders who had failed to lead, showed that the trade union movement, when it had time to think things over, realised that it had in effect made a challenge to the basis of British society which it was not prepared to see through and that, therefore, post-mortems on who was to blame were unprofitable. The industrial workers forgave their leaders. But they did not so easily forgive their enemies, particularly when the government, to punish them for their insubordination, rushed through the 1927 Trade Union Act. This did not, because it could not, prevent strikes: what it did was to make it more easy to victimise local strike leaders and also to put obstacles in the way of the unions contributing to the funds of their own political party.

(a) Why, according to Margaret Cole, did industrial workers after the General Strike forgive their trade union leaders but not government?

(b) What was the role of the press in forming and directing public opinion in the summer of 1926?

(c) Lord Grey, writing in the *British Gazette* in May 1926, said of the General Strike that 'It is an attempted revolution'. How far do the events of the summer of 1926, and subsequent actions of government and unions, support this view?

[Edexcel question]

Answers

(1) **Key issue: Using a primary source to examine the 1926 General Strike.**

Examiner's tip

Use only the source to answer (a). Use only your knowledge to answer (b). Use both the source and your own knowledge to answer (c).

(a) • Source shows that trade union leaders were forgiven because there were no feelings of revenge for their ineffective leadership. Strikers realised that the strike raised issues that were more extreme than the strikers wanted.

   • Government remained unpopular. Continued to punish the trade unionists by a harsh law in 1927 which was thought unfair. Leaders of the strike suffered. The Act tried to break the link between the trade unions and the Labour Party which the government believed to be an undemocratic situation.

(b) • Government used the press skilfully to explain the dangers in the strike and publicise any incidents which would discredit the strikers. The *British Gazette* claimed to publish accurate news but was used as propaganda to show that life was proceeding normally and the strikers were unreasonable or revolutionaries. Most newspapers were also against the strike.

   • The *British Worker* was less influential in putting the strikers' viewpoint. It had fewer resources and was less widely read.

   • Popular newspapers became more important in the early twentieth century but reflected rather than shaped or directed public opinion. Little evidence that the press changed opinions in the General Strike.

(c) • Grey's view is unjustified. Leaders and supporters of the General Strike did not aim at a revolution but wished to improve pay and working conditions. However, his statement was typical of those who wished to discredit the strikers.

   • Although it was called a General Strike, it was centred on the coal miners. Moderate trade union leaders were cautious about giving it their support.

   • Strike was led by moderate socialists rather than by communists or syndicalists who were more common on the continent. Trade unions rejected money that was sent from Russia. Few violent incidents and relations between strikers and police were generally good.

   • Government used propaganda to exaggerate the aims of the strikers. Source: The 1927 Trade Union Act was an unnecessary measure. Industrial workers gave more support to the Labour Party rather than to revolutionary groups.

Questions with model answers

C grade candidate – mark scored 6/10

 For help: See Revise AS Modern British and European History Study Guide pages 76–81

Examiner's Commentary

(a) *Explain how the Labour governments attempted to carry out their domestic policies from 1945 to 1951.*

The Labour government in 1945 aimed to carry out the most thorough changes in domestic policies ever attempted in Britain. It was believed that the economic problems and the harsh living conditions of the 1930s should never be allowed to return. The civilian population as well as soldiers, sailors and airman also deserved a better Britain after the sacrifices of the war. A ruined economy, the shortage of houses, poverty and an unfair education system were powerful reasons why extensive reforms were necessary ✔.

> Good introduction, explaining Labour's aims in 1945.

The major policies which were pursued by the Labour governments included the nationalisation of major industries to make them more efficient by bringing them under state control. The National Health Service was set up and a new National Insurance scheme was introduced. Education was reformed and more houses were built ✗.

> Answer describes major reforms but does not explain them sufficiently.

By 1951 the Labour government had become unpopular because of continuing shortages especially in food and housing. The Conservative party now promised to be able to deal with shortages more successfully and had overcome its unpopularity in 1945 ✗.

> Conclusion goes beyond what the question requires. No marks are given for irrelevance.

(b) *Assess the success of the Conservative governments from 1951 to 1964 in implementing **at least three** of their domestic policies.*

[OCR question]

The Conservatives soon ended food rationing as they had promised. Macmillan had already been a successful Minister of Housing and the Conservatives became popular as more people moved into better-equipped houses ✔.

> Good – a relevant introduction.

The end of food rationing was also popular and soon the electorate was convinced that they had `never had it so good´. More consumer goods such as cars and television sets were sold ✔.

> References to some domestic policies gets marks.

The success of the Conservatives was shown when they won three successive elections, in 1951, 1955 and 1959 but by 1964 they faced a better organised Labour party whose leader, Wilson, had new ideas. Scandals discredited the government and Macmillan's successor, Home, was an unpopular choice as leader of the Conservatives ✗.

> Paragraph is relevant but vague about the question.

The Conservatives were less successful abroad. Eden was responsible for the Suez crisis in 1956 and an attempt to join the European Economic Community failed. Britain's power in the world also declined as more colonies gained their independence ✗.

> Question is about domestic policies. This paragraph is not relevant.

Questions with model answers

A grade candidate – mark scored 8/10

For help: See Revise AS Modern British and European History Study Guide page 78

Examiner's Commentary

Why did British governments from 1945 to 1963 follow policies of decolonisation?

There were domestic and external reasons for the widespread decolonisation in the British Empire after the Second World War. The Labour party was less imperialist than the Conservatives whilst the shape of the Empire had changed since the beginning of the century with Australia, Canada and New Zealand becoming more independent. India was also given more powers of self-government in the inter-war period ✔.

Useful introduction about earlier moves towards decolonisation.

It was clear that Britain did not have the international power to control an empire. Domestic pressures, especially the need to rebuild after the Second World war, made the empire less of a priority for most people. International developments were important because other European countries were adopting similar policies whilst nationalist movements were growing in the colonies ✔.

Clear outline of varied reasons.

The first and most important move towards decolonisation was the independence of India in 1947. Although there was violence with the partition of India and Pakistan, the policy was supported by all British politicians except a few right-wing Conservatives. The term `Commonwealth´ rather than `Empire´ was adopted to reflect the changing relationship between Britain and other countries. From 1945 to 1963 Labour and Conservative governments followed very similar policies towards decolonisation. Left-wingers who wished to move more quickly and right-wingers who still had imperialist attitudes were in a minority. Attlee´s Labour Party led decolonisation after 1945 and Macmillan gave his speech about `a wind of change´ in Africa in 1960 after the Conservatives continued the process.

Indian independence was inevitable because of the rising tide of nationalism and Africa was the next continent where nationalism became a powerful force. The independence of west African states took place mostly in a peaceful manner. Nkrumah led the demand for independence in Ghana, which was achieved in 1957. A nationalist movement in Nigeria led to its agreed independence in 1960 followed by the smaller countries of Sierra Leone and Gambia. However, the pattern was different in east and central Africa. A larger white minority and racial divisions in Kenya resulted in civil war and terrorism by the Mau Mau. Attempts by the British government to suppress the troubles by force failed and Kenya became independent in 1963. Britain tried to enforce a federation on Nyasaland, northern and southern Rhodesia but this was unpopular because it was thought that it would dominated by white Rhodesians. By 1963, southern Rhodesia was on the verge of declaring its unilateral and illegal independence.

Analysis, not narrative, of Africa gets a high mark.

A grade candidate continued

For help: See Revise AS Modern British and European History Study Guide page 78

Examiner's Commentary

Federation was also attempted in the West Indies to help the islands to co-operate with each other. It failed and Jamaica and Trinidad and Tobago, the largest islands, became independent by 1962, soon followed by Barbados. However, the failure did not harm relations with Britain, which continued to have responsibility for the smaller islands ✔.

Decolonisation was mostly carried out with the consent of British governments. The Commonwealth, with the British monarchy at its head, represented a new relationship between Britain and its former colonies.

Answer deals with a range of regions.

Exam practice question

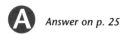 *Answer on p. 25*

(1) Source-based question: Britain's international situation in 1947

Read the following source and then answer the questions which follow.

From An Ocean Apart, *by David Dimbleby and David Reynolds, 1988.*

In February 1947, the Cabinet accepted that the country was over-stretched and decided to cut back on Britain's spending overseas. This meant pulling out of Palestine, India, Greece and Turkey. Notes were delivered to Washington explaining the new policy and asking for more financial assistance. On March 12th, President Truman addressed Congress, setting out the 'Truman Doctrine'.

(a)   What is meant by the term 'Truman Doctrine' in relation to the events of 1947?

(b)   Explain in what ways Britain's economic situation was 'over-stretched' in February 1947.

(c)   In what ways did the relationship between Britain and the United States between the end of the war and March 1947 reflect the weakening of Britain's position as a world power?

[AQA question]

Answers

(1)   **Key issue: Using a secondary source to examine Britain's relationship with the United States in 1947.**

Examiner's tip

(a) should be answered briefly. Use the source and your own knowledge to answer (b) and (c).

(a) • USA believed that there was a strong Soviet communist threat to democracy in Europe after the Second World War. By 1947, the USSR controlled much of eastern Europe. Other European governments might not be able to defend themselves alone against this threat.

   • The Truman Doctrine gave economic and military help to European countries. Later extended to anti-communist countries in the rest of the world.

   • It was linked to the Marshall Plan, also announced in 1947, which offered financial aid.

(b) • The war destroyed much of the British economy, which had to be reconstructed. Considerable national debt; loans were owed to the USA. Source shows that Britain was already receiving financial help from the USA by 1947. Rationing, price controls and currency regulations were enforced. Food subsidies were expensive for the government. The severe winter in 1947 disrupted the economy further.

   • Stafford Cripps, the Chancellor of the Exchequer, pursued a policy of austerity because of the poor economic situation.

   • Labour government's nationalisation of major industries and the planned introduction of the National Health Service were thought necessary but strained the economy.

   • Source gives examples of regions to which Britain was committed after the Second World War. Indian independence agreed (1947). Britain was also involved in the Middle East and elsewhere. The war added to the existing pressures to reduce Britain's world commitments.

(c) • Second World War had shown that the USA had become the more powerful partner in the alliance, militarily and economically. Churchill and Attlee attended the conferences at Yalta and Potsdam but the American Presidents Roosevelt and Truman were much more important in the negotiations with Stalin. After the war, Britain was clearly the junior partner in the alliance with the USA. The world was divided into the Big Two rather than the Big Three.

   • British government's message to the USA in February 1947 confirmed the developments since 1945. The Cold War saw the USA lead the defence of democracy against the USSR. American Lend-Lease had been vital for Britain's survival since 1941. Britain lost many of its export markets.

   • USA gave financial and economic aid to Europe immediately after the war. The Truman Doctrine continued this policy. USA was the only country that could rival the military power of the USSR.

   • Britain also had other overseas commitments that are not referred to in the source, for example its other colonies, and these added to its problems. Britain wished to remain the centre of a powerful empire, independent of the USA. This was impossible as decolonisation developed.

Questions with model answers

 For help: See Revise AS Modern British and European History Study Guide pages 83–84

C grade candidate – mark scored 6/10

What were the aims of the 'Ultras' in France?

[CCEA question]

Examiner's Commentary

The Ultras were the extreme royalists in France who supported the policies of Charles X. Many of them were émigrés who had left France after the outbreak of the revolution in 1789. They wanted to turn back the clock and wished to restore conditions of the ancien régime before the French Revolution, favouring a strong monarchy ✔.

Answer is relevant and concentrates on explanation.

The Ultras disliked the Charter, which had been granted by Louis XVIII. They wanted ministers who were in favour of absolute government to replace moderates. They favoured the restoration to the aristocracy of land which had been confiscated and a stronger role for the Catholic Church because they were less tolerant than the moderates in France. The Church, not the state, should control education. As a result, Charles X's aims and policies were very unpopular in France and led to a revolution in 1830 ✗.

The period from 1815 must be explained more fully. The discussion of the Ultras during the reign of Louis XVIII is thin.

(1) Ultras wished to punish republicans, Bonapartists and liberals.

(2) Charles X - rule by divine right, not by the will of the French people.

(3) The Chamber should obey him. Dismissed it when opposition grew ✗.

Avoid notes. They get fewer marks than continuous prose. Take care with time management.

A grade candidate – mark scored 8/10

How acceptable is the view that the Congress System was successful as an exercise in Great Power co-operation in the period 1815 to 1825? Explain your answer.

[AQA question]

The Vienna settlement (1815) agreed the peace terms which followed the defeat of Napoleon and laid the foundations of the Congress System. The most important countries which had defeated France, Austria, Britain, Prussia and Russia, signed a Quadruple Alliance and agreed to meet regularly to preserve the peace. Such meetings took place at Aix-la-Chappelle (1818), Troppau (1820), Laibach (1821) and Verona (1822). Only three members attended a Congress at St. Petersburg in 1825. From 1815 to 1825 there was no major war in Europe and it seemed as if the Congress System demonstrated international co-operation but there were many tensions between the major powers, which led to the end of the congresses ✔.

Good introduction. Highlights the main argument in the answer.

A grade candidate continued

For help: See Revise AS Modern British and European History Study Guide pages 40–41

Examiner's Commentary

The statesmen had co-operated at Vienna to make sure that France would no longer be a threat. At the Congress of Aix-la-Chappelle, France joined the Quintuple Alliance although the Quadruple Alliance of other countries was secretly renewed as an insurance. Austria, Prussia and Russia had competing interests in Germany and eastern Europe whilst Britain was more concerned with its interests at sea in the rest of the world. Britain was a more democratic country whereas autocratic and anti-liberal rulers governed the three others. Austria and Russia especially were concerned about the danger of nationalist and liberal movements after the French Revolution and the Napoleonic wars. Russia was keen to intervene to crush rebellions against kings, for example in Spain, Portugal and Italy ✔.

Analytical approach is better than narrative.

The Troppau Protocol (1820) stated that Austria, Prussia and Russia had the right to make war on revolutions and Austria suppressed revolts in Naples and Piedmont. The Tsar was willing to send a Russian army to Spain, which even Metternich of Austria opposed. Castlereagh, Britain's Foreign Secretary, disliked such intervention in the affairs of other countries. He already distrusted the Holy Alliance and issued a paper in 1820, which rejected the Troppau Protocol.

There was less co-operation at the Congress of Verona, which Castlereagh did not attend personally. The meeting was divided over intervention in Spain. Britain and Austria opposed the move but France was willing to support Russia. There were disagreements about recognising the independence of Spanish colonies in the Americas. The outbreak of the Greek Revolt (1821) emphasised the differences between the major powers. Russia was strongly in favour of helping the Greeks but Britain feared growing Russian power in the Mediterranean although there was some sympathy with the Greeks. The rivalries between European countries were clear by 1825 and the Congress System had broken down. Nevertheless, the main aim in 1815 had been achieved because France was integrated peacefully into European affairs ✔.

Answer concentrates on issues between the major countries. Examines the key issues.

Exam practice questions

Answers on p. 29

(1) (a)   Explain the aims of Louis Philippe in domestic and foreign affairs.

(b)   How justified is the claim that the most important reason for the fall of Louis Philippe was social and economic distress?

(2) (a)   Explain the reasons why Napoleon III was able to establish the Second Empire by 1852.

(b)   Compare the importance of at least **three** factors in the downfall of the Second Empire.

[OCR question]

Answers

(1) (a)   Key issue: Explanation of domestic and foreign aims of Louis Philippe.

Examiner's tip

Write a balanced account of domestic and foreign aims. Avoid narrative of the reign.
Give examples to illustrate his aims.

- Introduction: Louis Philippe – the 'Citizen King' because of his election after the 1830 Revolution and his moderate manner. Constitution was similar to the Charter of 1814. Title was King by 'the grace of God' – traditional, and by 'the will of the people' – new. Louis Philippe respected Lafayette, popular republican hero, and adopted the tricolour flag. Won the support of the National Guard.
- Domestic aims: The electorate was expanded but he did not want universal suffrage. Relied on middle classes who had brought him to power. Guizot a conservative minister. Resisted demands that the vote should be given to the working classes. Censorship abolished. Juries could try more cases. Authority of the Roman Catholic Church was weakened.
- Economic aims: Free trade and industry encouraged. Helped manufacturers. Did not benefit the working classes and farmers, who preferred protectionism.
- Foreign aims: Did not want France to return to the dangerous days of Napoleon when the country had many enemies in Europe. War was expensive and would divide France. His aims were less ambitious and exciting than some Frenchmen wished. Agreed to co-operate with Britain over Belgium and Middle East.

(b)   Key issue: Assessment of most important reasons for fall of Louis Philippe.

Examiner's tip

Organise the answer, putting your most important reasons first. Discuss the variety of groups opposed to the King. Explain the 1848 Revolution.

- Radicals and republicans: Continued to agitate and cause uprisings, for example in Paris and Lyons in the early 1830s. Blanqui formed a secret society. Unrest in the army.
- Economic policy: Free trade helped middle classes but weakened workers. Economic conditions became worse during the 1840s. Workers in large cities were attracted by more revolutionary ideas. Socialism began to spread. Louis Blanc believed that all men had a right to work. Organised workshops from which workers could receive a share of the income. Proudhon claimed that all private property should be abolished.
- Unpopular government: Guizot was unwilling to introduce reforms to improve the situation. By 1848, a dangerous coalition of workers, socialists, republicans and Bonapartists (supporters of Louis Napoleon). Guizot's dismissal did not save Louis Philippe. Paris was again the centre of a revolution. Uncontrolled riots. National Guard turned against the King.

Answers

(2) (a) **Key issue: Explanation of reasons for establishment of Second Empire.**

Examiner's tip

Focus on 1852, connecting developments from 1848 to the coup d'état. Examine Louis Napoleon's aims and policies. Consider the weakness of the opposition.

- Establishment of the Empire: Louis Napoleon established the Second Empire with an autocratic government in 1852. Violence and extremism of the 1848 radicals alarmed many people in France. Louis Napoleon promised order and peace. The June Days – the army suppressed disorder by force.
- Support: Louis Napoleon promised to unite the nation. Nephew of Napoleon Bonaparte and might restore the greatness of France as a European country. His books, such as *The Elimination of Pauperism*, gained the support of the poor. Royalists preferred him to a republican leader. Louis Napoleon won a massive majority in the presidential election in 1848 and gained even more power in 1852.
- Presidential powers: He could appoint ministers, leaders of the army and National Guard. One of the first European politicians to use propaganda effectively.
- Popular appeal: Plebiscites used to gain support for his proposals and to avoid opposition in the National Assembly. Louis Napoleon announced that he was in favour of universal suffrage. The National Assembly wished to limit the franchise.
- Foreign affairs: More active foreign policy than Louis Philippe. Intervention to protect the Pope against Mazzini's Roman Republic was popular.
- 1852 coup: Constitution allowed the President one term of four years in office. Louis Napoleon toured the provinces to win support. Changed the law by force in a coup d'état (1851). Army supported him. Leaders of the opposition were arrested. Plebiscite recorded a large majority in his favour.

(b) **Key issue: Comparison of three reasons for fall of Second Empire.**

Examiner's tip

Comparison should be organised, showing similarities and differences. Consider reasons in order of importance. Focus on 1870–71, relating earlier developments to these years.

- Defeat in war: Fall of the Second Empire followed France's defeat by Prussia at Sedan (1870). Napoleon III was outwitted by Bismarck and failed in other foreign policies in 1860s. After the Ems Telegram, pressure grew in France for a war with Prussia. The humiliation of Sedan, after previous failures in foreign policy, caused the collapse of the government.
- Opposition in France: Empire had become more liberal during the 1860s. The Assembly had become more influential. Debates were published; opponents were allowed to sit. Censorship was relaxed. Changes did not strengthen Napoleon III's government but he still had considerable power and remained personally popular. Won a plebiscite in 1870 before the war with Prussia. Critics (Ollivier) had to be used as ministers and this divided the government when Napoleon III was negotiating with Bismarck. Public opinion pressed for war.
- Economic reasons: Social unrest. Worsening economic conditions affected the working classes. Radicals and republicans were more influential after Napoleon III was defeated.

Questions with model answers

C grade candidate – mark scored 6/10

 For help: See Revise AS Modern British and European History Study Guide pages 91–92

Examine the condition of Russia at the accession of Alexander II.

[OCR question]

Alexander II acceded to the Russian throne in 1855 in the middle of the Crimean War. Russia fought against Britain, France and Turkey because it hoped to partition Turkish territory and extend its influence in the Mediterranean. The war went badly and Alexander II had to agree to the Peace of Paris (1856). Russia had to make many concessions in this treaty ✗

The Tsar believed that serfdom should be abolished because it had caused the defeat of Russia in the war. The Russian army was unwieldy and badly trained. Russia needed a more professional and well-trained army. Better recruits and training would be possible if the serfs were emancipated. There were peasant risings during the war, which prevented the government from concentrating on fighting the enemy. Alexander II's predecessor, Nicholas I, had believed that serfdom should be ended but had not carried this policy out in practice. There had been frequent peasant rebellions and serfs were an inefficient way of organising agriculture. They also prevented industrial changes because they were tied to the land and Russia needed more factory workers ✔.

However, many nobles and even some peasants opposed emancipation. Nobles resisted the idea and the Tsar's advisers thought that it would be too difficult. Peasants believed that the land, which they worked, was already theirs ✗.

Examiner's Commentary

Narrative of war instead of focus on key issue of condition of Russia. What does the war tell us about the key issue?

Good explanation of the problem of serfdom.

Important gaps in explanation, for example autocratic government. Answer is too limited for a high mark.

Questions with model answers

A grade candidate – mark scored 8/10

 For help: See Revise AS Modern British and European History Study Guide pages 91–92

Why did the reforms of Alexander II not make him a more popular tsar?

Examiner's Commentary

Although Alexander II was given the title of `Tsar Liberator´ because of the emancipation of the serfs (1861), his policies did not make him popular with all Russians. Some believed that his reforms had not gone far enough whilst others believed that he went too far. His lack of popularity was shown after 1866 when he seemed to change from reformer to reactionary. Extremists such as the anarchists and The People´s Will caused violence and revolutionaries assassinated the Tsar ✔.

Immediate discussion of key issue.

The emancipation of the serfs was a major change for Russia because serfdom was so inefficient but many of the serfs remained dissatisfied. They received small plots of land, often of poor quality, for which they had to pay redemption fees over 49 years. The prices that they were charged were often higher than the land was worth. The mirs now had a lot of control over their lives. Many could not afford the repayments and left the land for the towns where conditions were no better. There were strikes in the large cities. The nobles lost their rights and land and expressed their dissatisfaction to Alexander II. The zemstvos were intended to be local assemblies in which nobles and others could play a part but they had few powers. Education, which was encouraged by the Tsar, created a class of dissatisfied people who wanted further changes. Censorship was eased and allowed the spread of critical books and newspapers ✔.

Analytical approach that considers a variety of policies deserves a high mark.

A revolt in Poland (1863) was followed by the violence and the threat of revolution. The Tsar´s reputation as a reformer suffered when secret courts and the police were used to deal with the opposition. The universities were controlled more tightly. Censorship became harsher. There were hundreds of trials and many were imprisoned or exiled to Siberia. The government received little support from these measures. The conservatives in Russia blamed the Tsar´s policies for causing the trouble whilst opposition from the liberals and revolutionaries grew even more ✔.

Deals with a range of opposition groups.

Just before his assassination (1881), Alexander considered changing back to a more reforming manner. He was willing to relax censorship and allow more power to the zemstvos but it was too late to win widespread popularity. Although Alexander liberated the serfs and introduced other reforms, he remained an autocrat and was unwilling to change the basic systems of government and society ✔.

Well-organised answer with good introduction and conclusion.

Exam practice questions

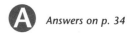

Answers on p. 34

(1) **(a)** What do you understand by the Eastern Question in the period 1821 to 1856? Explain your answer.

(b) How far were Russian policies responsible for instability in the Balkans from 1856 to 1914?

(2) **(a)** Explain the victory of the Bolsheviks in the period 1917 to 1921.

(b) How far had Lenin achieved his aims at the time of his death in 1924?

Answers

(1) (a)   Key issue: Explanation of the Eastern Question.

Examiner's tip

Analyse the different issues involved in the question. Avoid vagueness but note the specified dates.

- Rivalry between Turkey and Russia: Turkish Empire was widespread and included Balkan states. Muslim, but many of the inhabitants of the Balkans were Orthodox Christian. Nationalism spread and Balkan states such as Greece wanted to be independent. By 1821, Turkey was weak and inefficient. Russia's ambition was to spread into the Mediterranean through the Dardanelles, which were controlled by Turkey. Claimed to be the protector of the fellow Orthodox Christians and Slavs in the Balkans.
- British policy: Britain wished to preserve the Turkish Empire. Russia would be a danger to its trade and empire if it expanded into the Mediterranean. Some sympathy for the Balkan people but this was usually less important than fears of Russia.
- French policy: France particularly concerned about the Eastern Question during the reign of Napoleon III. Wanted France to play an important role in European affairs. Opposed Russia's claim to protect the Holy Places.
- Austrian policy: Austria, led by Metternich to 1848, governed parts of the Balkans. Feared that partition of the Turkish Empire might lead to rebellions in its own empire.
- Key developments: Greece won the War of Independence (1821–29). Russia sought an agreement from Turkey in 1830s to allow its warships to sail into the Mediterranean. Angered other European countries who forced it to agree in the Straits Convention (1841) – Dardanelles closed to all warships. The Crimean War (1854–56) broke out when Russia continued to claim rights against Turkey. Eastern Question ended the European peace since 1815.

(b)   Key issue: Assessment of the reasons for instability in the Balkans.

Examiner's tip

Discuss first Russia's responsibility. Compare the importance of other factors.

- Russia's aims: Russia was ally of the Balkan peoples. Encouraged them to rebel against Turkey. Defeat in the Crimean War was humiliating; the Balkans were an opportunity to extend its influence.
- Austria-Hungary's aims: Russia was opposed by Austria-Hungary, which wished to suppress Balkan nationalism. By 1914, these two countries were enemies. Austria-Hungary joined Germany and Italy in the Triple Alliance. Russia was in the Triple Entente with Britain and France. Instability in the Balkans spread dangerously to other parts of Europe.
- Instability in the Balkans: Many Balkan states wished to become independent from Turkish rule. Rumania became independent in 1875 and Bulgaria in 1878. Conferences, for example the Congress of Berlin (1878), failed to solve the problem. Turkey attacked by Bulgaria, Greece, Montenegro and Serbia in the Balkans War (1912).

- Serbia's role: Serbia wished to be the leading Balkan state. In conflict with Austria. Terrorist groups against Austria-Hungary, for example the 'Black Hand', were based in Serbia and were responsible for the assassination of Archduke Franz Ferdinand at Sarajevo, which began the First World War.

(2) (a)   Key issue: Explanation of the victory of the Bolsheviks.

Examiner's tip

Concentrate on explanation and avoid narrative. Focus on the specified years 1917–21.

- Kerensky's provisional government was discredited; continued with the unsuccessful war. Lenin promised 'Peace, Land and Bread', the priorities of the Russian masses. Agreed the harsh Treaty of Brest-Litovsk with Germany.
- Lenin a decisive and ruthless leader. Bolsheviks were well-organised, controlling the Red Army and the soviets. Constituent Assembly was dispersed. Single-party state was established. Police silenced the opposition.
- Bolsheviks won the Civil War against the Whites. Trotsky led the Red Army; Lenin gave political leadership. This was more effective than their divided enemies. Intervention of other countries on behalf of the Whites made the Bolsheviks appear as the defenders of Russian independence.
- Ruthless terrorism and harsh economic measures (confiscated land and industries) crushed internal opposition to the Bolsheviks.

(b)   Key issue: Assessment of Lenin's success.

Examiner's tip

This question asks 'How far?'. You should consider the extent of Lenin's success and failure. Make clear which you think was more important.

- Lenin's aims: To establish a one-party Marxist state. In theory, it would be the dictatorship of the proletariat, leading to a classless state. Power would be held by the Bolsheviks. Capitalism, with the private ownership of business, would disappear.
- Lenin's achievements: By 1924, the Bolsheviks were firmly in power. One-party state. Bolshevik government had survived civil and foreign war. Economy was improving after civil war and famine. Lenin's leadership was unchallenged. He was universally recognised as the founder of the modern Russian state.
- Lenin's failures: Lenin's War Communism failed; replaced by the New Economic Policy (NEP), which encouraged private profit and was a move away from communism. Government was controlled by a few people. Proletariat was excluded from power. Lenin's ill health from 1923 weakened his hold and his death was followed by a disputed succession. He probably did not wish Stalin to succeed him.

Questions with model answers

C grade candidate – mark scored 6/10

 For help: See Revise AS Modern British and European History Study Guide pages 132–133

Why was Italy not completely unified until 1871?

[Edexcel question]

Examiner's Commentary

There were demands for a united Italy since at least 1815 when the Vienna settlement restored former rulers and divided Italy into small states, most of which were under the influence of Austria. Revolts continued until 1848 but the revolutionaries failed to achieve a united Italy. They were divided in their aims. Mazzini supported a democratic and unified republic. Gioberti favoured a federation of Italian states under the leadership of the Pope. Charles Albert of Piedmont-Sardinia wished to lead a monarchy in northern Italy. Lacking unity and with weak armies, the revolutionaries were crushed by Austria.

Cavour learned the lessons of 1848. In spite of its defeat, Piedmont was the most important Italian state. It had a comparatively liberal constitution and a better economy which Cavour helped to strengthen. The support of King Victor Emmanuel was important. However, Cavour initially did not wish to unify Italy. He aimed to expel Austria from Italy and extend Piedmont's influence over other northern states ✔.

Basic factors are explained satisfactorily.

Unexpected events won him a powerful ally in France. Napoleon III had previously sympathised with Italian nationalists although French troops were protecting the pope in Rome. Piedmont's role in the Crimean War has been exaggerated but Napoleon III was persuaded to support Cavour. After the Pact of Plombières, the French army helped Piedmont to defeat Austria at Magenta and Solferino. Although Napoleon III made a truce with Austria, Lombardy and Venetia came under Piedmontese control. Plebiscites in Tuscany, Emilia and the Romagna added to these territories ✗.

Lower marks are given for narrative than analysis.

Cavour's flexibility was shown when he agreed to surrender Nice and Savoy to France as the price of Napoleon III's assistance and when he went further than his original aims by taking advantage of Garibaldi's conquest of Naples and Sicily. He was careful not to try to integrate Rome, which would have angered France and other Catholic countries. The kingdom of Italy was set up in 1861 without Venetia and Rome ✗.

The answer takes a long time to get to the key period.

Cavour's death delayed further unification. His successors were not as skilful and there were disagreements between the nationalists. Venetia was gained in 1866 when Italy assisted Prussia in its war with Austria. The final unification of Rome was also the indirect result of a war between other countries. Napoleon III was forced to withdraw the French garrison in Rome and Italian troops marched in unopposed. After a plebiscite, Rome became the capital of Rome. Therefore, after steady progress under Cavour, unification was delayed until 1871 because of the weakness of the nationalists and their dependence on the outcomes of foreign wars ✔.

Satisfactory explanation of developments after 1861.

A grade candidate – mark scored 8/10

For help: See Revise AS Modern British and European History Study Guide pages 108–109

Examiner's Commentary

To what extent did Bismarck control the process of German unification?

[WJEC question]

It was impossible for any politician to control events over a period of ten years, even one who was as capable as Bismarck. Prussia was the most important German state but there were others which were proud of their independence and Austria had a larger influence in Germany than Prussia. Historians disagree about the extent to which Bismarck wished to unify Germany. Most now believe that his most important priority was to extend Prussia's influence, especially over the north German states. Unification and the creation of the German Empire in 1871 were the results of unforeseen circumstances of which Bismarck took advantage ✔.

Analytical approach focuses on the key issue.

Bismarck did not create crises but was willing to exploit them and risk war to gain advantages for Prussia. To a large extent, the wars with Denmark, Austria and France began with crises that originated outside Prussia. They depended as much on other countries as on Prussia.

Although Bismarck led the movement for unification, his work depended on others. Prussia had a strong economy and the Zollverein, which excluded Austria, gave it economic leadership over other German states. Keynes claimed that unity resulted more from coal and iron than blood and iron. The Prussian army was the largest in Europe and three wars against Denmark, Austria and France showed that it was the most powerful in Europe. It had been developed especially by Roon and von Moltke and Bismarck's decisive actions in 1862 in collecting taxes for the army against the opposition of Prussian liberals won him support from William I and the powerful military. The growing weakness of Austria was crucial. It had been the dominating force in Germany since 1815 and helped to crush the 1848 Revolutions. The Olmütz Convention (1852) confirmed Austria's power. However, defeat against Piedmont and the loss of Russia's friendship after the Crimean War weakened Austria. Support for a Little Germany (Kleindeutschland) grew as support for Great Germany, including Austria (Grossdeutschland) declined ✔.

Considers alternative explanations.

Bismarck was willing to gamble but only when he had made sure that the stakes were heavily in his favour. The constitutional crisis over the budget secured his position in Prussia. He won Austria's support in the war with Denmark, then made allies of Italy, France and Russia when he turned on Austria. He believed correctly that Britain would not intervene. France was isolated by 1870 and Bismarck's use of the Ems Telegram showed his ruthlessness, even when William I wished to take a more moderate line. He did not control any of these events but he had considerable insight into how others would react to his policies ✔.

Avoids narrative. Uses facts to support the argument.

Exam practice question

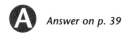

Answer on p. 39

(1) Source-based question: Bismarck 1871–90

Read the following source and answer the questions which follow.

From Europe Transformed, *by N. Stone.*

> After the crucial events of 1878–1879, Bismarck maintained complete Conservative
> dominance in Germany, supported by the alliance of 'Steel and Rye', and was able
> to virtually ignore the opposition from liberals, Catholics and Socialists.

(a)   What was meant by the 'alliance of Steel and Rye'?

(b)   Explain why the events of 1878–1879 were so significant for the internal
political affairs of Germany.

(c)   'The internal strengths of imperial Germany outweighed its weaknesses at
the time of the fall of Bismarck.' Explain why you agree or disagree with this
statement.

[AQA question]

Answers

(1)   **Key issue: Explanation of Bismarck after the unification of Germany.**

Examiner's tip

Use the source as stimulus to frame your answers. You must also use your own knowledge.

(a) • Steel: Refers to the new industrialists who made Germany very prosperous and had considerable economic, political and social power. Opposed regulations on industry.
- Rye: Older Prussian junkers were based on agriculture, signified by rye. Politically conservative.
- Alliance: These groups did not have much in common. Their backgrounds were very different. But they had common enemies: liberals who wanted economic and political reform, Catholics who seemed to have loyalties outside Protestant Germany, Socialists who supported industrial and political changes.

(b) • Kulturkampf: Bismarck believed that the papacy claimed too much power for the Roman Catholic Church over the State. The Roman Catholic Centre Party seemed a threat to a Protestant-dominated Germany. The Kulturkampf (anti-Catholic measures) reached a stalemate. Election of Pope Leo XIII enabled Bismarck to restore relations with the papacy.
- Anti-socialism: Socialists were seen as a political, economic and social danger. Bismarck introduced anti-socialist laws. Labour groups and political and economic organisations suppressed. Socialist publications banned. Socialists blamed unfairly for attempts to assassinate Kaiser William I. Support for the Socialists increased and Bismarck had to modify his policies later.
- End of free trade: 1871– Bismarck sided with the liberals in 1871 when he needed their support in the new Germany. 1879 – adopted protectionism rather than free trade which the liberals favoured. Bismarck gained support of industrialists and farming interests.

(c)   Internal strengths:
- Bismarck gave the newly united Germany almost 20 years of comparatively stable government.
- German economy grew faster than any other European country, especially modern iron, steel, electrical and chemical industries. Exports boomed. Railways spread. Protectionism helped agriculture.
- The German army was the most powerful in Europe.

Internal weaknesses:
- William II was unstable and unpredictable, which was dangerous because of the considerable power of the Kaiser. Officer corps was authoritarian and had an important political role in Germany. It was supported by the Kaiser.
- Social tensions weakened Germany. Socialists increased in number and Bismarck had to revise anti-socialist laws to cope with unrest.

Conclusion:
- Germany was apparently stable in 1890 but Bismarck's policies, although successful during his period of office, led to considerable problems in the future.

Questions with model answers

C grade candidate – mark scored 6/10

 For help: See Revise AS Modern British and European History Study Guide pages 135–138

Explain the weaknesses of the Weimar Republic to 1933.

Examiner's Commentary

The Weimar Republic was set up in 1919 after Germany's defeat in the First World War. Its establishment was the result of military defeat and it was blamed unfairly for the concessions which were forced on Germany in the post-war settlements. Germany lost Alsace-Lorraine and parts of Poland. The Saar was occupied by France for fifteen years and the Rhineland was demilitarised. The size of the army and navy was reduced to a minimum and the air force was dismantled. Overseas colonies were lost. Very heavy reparations had to be paid to the victors and Germany had to accept the War Guilt Clause ✗.

> Unnecessary details about the post-war settlement.

The amount of reparations was far more than Germany could afford but France was determined that they should be paid and occupied the Ruhr in 1923 when the Weimar government announced that it could not pay. The result was hyper-inflation and massive unemployment. Wages and savings became worthless as prices soared. American loans and agreements such as the Dawes and Young Plans eased Germany's problems and Stresemann, the Foreign Minister from 1923 to 1929, helped to stabilise the situation by winning the co-operation of other countries. Germany signed the Locarno Pact, accepting the post-war frontiers, and joined the League of Nations, becoming a permanent member of the Council as a major country. His death coincided with the Wall Street Crash which hit Germany particularly hard because it depended so much on American investments. Unemployment increased and the Weimar Republic was blamed again for conditions which were mostly outside its control ✔.

> Good section on the economic problems of Weimar.

Hitler became the leader of the Nazi party in the early 1920s and it attracted support from ex-soldiers who were bitter about Germany's defeat in the First World War and from other political extremists. The Munich Putsch was a failure but gave Hitler a reputation as an enemy of the Weimar Republic and he wrote Mein Kampf, the Nazi programme. After this, he re-organised the Nazi party and aimed to gain more political support in the Reichstag. At the same time, the SA was used to terrorise unpopular groups such as the Jews ✗.

> Need for more analysis of hostility to Weimar, for example right wing, big business, military.

By 1930, the Nazis were the second largest political group. The other political parties could not agree on measures to cope with the economic problem and proportional representation meant that no single party had a majority. Hitler refused to serve under another Chancellor. In the end, President Hindenburg appointed Hitler when it was thought that he could be controlled by other politicians. The Reichstag Fire was wrongly blamed on communists and gave Hitler the opportunity to pass the Enabling Law in 1933. The Weimar Republic had lost any effective support and Germany turned into a Nazi dictatorship ✔.

> Good account of the fall of Weimar to the Nazis.

A grade candidate – mark scored 8/10

For help: See Revise AS Modern British and European History Study Guide pages 138–146

The Nazis in the 1930s.

Examiner's Commentary

'The Nazis were popular with the majority of Germans because they gave the people everything they wanted.' *Franz Neuman, a German economist who was forced to flee Germany in 1936, writing in an essay published in the United States, 1944.*

How valid is this interpretation of the reasons for the popularity of the Nazis during the 1930s?

[WJEC question]

Neuman was a critic of the Nazis who left Germany in the middle of the 1930s. The source was written towards the end of the Second World War in America, which was then the enemy of Germany. However, although he was not an objective writer, his interpretation is valid. Hitler and the Nazis had complete power in Germany but not only because their policies were designed to win maximum support. They suppressed all opposition and imposed totalitarian rule ✔.

Brief discussion of quotation in source.

Large industrialists co-operated and new labour unions, controlled by the Nazis, replaced independent trade unions. Unemployment was reduced because of public works, such as the building of autobahn, the creation of unnecessary offices and the dismissal of Jews and critics of the Nazis. Four-Year Plans gave priority to rearmament and industries which produced armaments prospered. This was particularly important to the military class and Hitler gained a higher reputation with the officers when he crushed the SA. Industrialists saw the Nazis as a defence against communism ✔.

Analytical approach deserves a high mark.

Hitler's aim to win back the concessions which were forced on Germany at the end of the First World War was welcomed by most Germans. The Saar was restored to Germany, the Rhineland was re-occupied and the Anschluss with Austria was declared. Hitler emphasised the claims of the German people in the Sudetenland when he seized Czechoslovakia.

Propaganda, co-ordinated by Goebbels, was important to the success of the Nazis. Rallies were arranged and public opinion was controlled. Radio, cinema and newspapers were dominated by the party and won support for the regime. At the same time, Hitler agreed a Concordat with the Roman Catholic Church and was supported by many Protestants. A few Catholic and Protestant priests who opposed the Nazis were unrepresentative of their Churches. Racial policies unified the Germans by emphasising their special role as a pure master

Questions with model answers

A grade candidate continued

 For help: See Revise AS Modern British and European History Study Guide pages 138–146

Examiner's Commentary

race which had a duty of destroy un-German groups such as the Jews and other minorities. Children and young people were indoctrinated in these ideas. Women were subordinated to men but this was explained by the theory that their particular responsibility was in the home ✔.

Varied and relevant points.

Propaganda concealed economic failures and described those arrested by the Gestapo as enemies of all Germans. Therefore the terror tactics of the regime were disguised as defences of the majority. Hitler's personal role as Führer made him the father as well as the master of the German people. Neuman was correct to claim that most Germans gained what they wanted but usually at the expense of others.

Considers alternative views.

Exam practice question

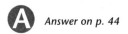 *Answer on p. 44*

(1) Source-based question: The rule of Stalin

Read the following source and then answer the questions which follow.

From Hope Against Hope, *by N. Mandelstam (who lived in the USSR in the 1930s), 1971.*

> My friend Sonia Vishnweski, hearing every day of new arrests among her friends, shouted in horror: 'Treachery and counter-revolution everywhere!'. This was how you were supposed to react if you lived in relative comfort and had something to lose.

(a)   Explain what was meant by 'counter-revolution' in the USSR in the 1930s.

(b)   Explain why Stalin accused so many people of 'treachery and counter-revolution' in the USSR in the 1930s.

(c)   Do you agree with the view that Stalin successfully removed 'treachery and counter-revolution' in the USSR in the 1930s? Explain your answer.

[AQA question]

Answers

(1)   **Key issue: Stalin and counter-revolution in the 1930s.**

Examiner's tip

Use the source to help you plan the answers but also use your own knowledge.

(a) • Counter-revolution originally meant any action against the 1917 revolution, for example from tsarist sympathisers, capitalists or foreign enemies.

• In the 1930s, Stalin widened the term to apply to anybody who was even suspected of being critical of his regime. Members of the military and former allies such as old Bolsheviks were accused of being counter-revolutionaries during the purges.

(b) • Stalin wished to achieve complete domination of the USSR. Possible or imagined rivals were purged, including those who had helped to bring him to power, government ministers and officials who ran the communist party. Stalin wanted to ensure that there were no alternative views to defeat his programme, for example Trotskyists or capitalists.

• Possible that Stalin feared the growing threat of Nazi Germany. Wished to make the USSR more secure and prevent a possible civil war. Many military officers were purged.

• Some historians believe that Stalin's personal and unreasonable suspicions were a major reason why so many were accused because most were innocent of any charges. Source shows the widespread fear that anybody could be arrested as a counter-revolutionary.

(c) • Source is an eye-witness account of conditions in the USSR at the time. Although written later, it is supported by other evidence that we have of conditions. Significant that the writer seems to have lived in comfort; this class was particularly attacked by Stalin.

• Stalin destroyed every other power base in the USSR: party, police, military and economic, for example Zinoviev, Kamenev, Bukharin, Yagoda and Tukachevsky. Kulaks regarded as traitors and counter-revolutionaries and disappeared as a class. Millions of them were killed. Industrial workers were terrorised. Gulags mostly filled with people who were guilty of minor crimes or who were completely innocent.

• No serious threat of treachery and counter-revolution. Confessions were forced. Show trials for the famous and punishment without trial for others are not evidence of treachery. Stalin whipped up rumours which the population had to repeat, as in the source.

• Results for the USSR were disastrous. Military was seriously weakened and the economy suffered. However, Stalin was successful in his aim of strengthening his own position and imposing his own brand of communism.

Questions with model answers

C grade candidate – mark scored 6/10

Assess the extent of the support for the monarchy during the period 1815–1910.

Examiner's Commentary

Republicanism was usually weak in nineteenth-century Britain, unlike some continental countries such as France and Italy where republicans played an important role throughout this period. There were several reasons for the weakness of republicanism and the support for the monarchy including the absence of extreme political groups. The British monarchy had limited powers when continental republicans opposed absolute rulers. Another important reason was that Victoria remained personally popular for most of her reign and her death resulted in considerable mourning ✔.

Good introduction that puts the question in context.

Queen Victoria succeeded to the throne in 1837 and her view that she should play an important part in politics caused problems. She supported Melbourne against Peel. Most famously, she admired Disraeli, who flattered her personally, consulted her and made her Empress of India, but disliked Gladstone, who she thought preached at her. Although she usually gave way, she could make difficulties for her ministers because she sometimes did not recognise the limits on a monarch's power in England ✔.

Good section on Victoria.

Although she withdrew from public life after the death of Albert, she still insisted on being consulted by her ministers who had to make long journeys to Balmoral in Scotland or Osborne House on the Isle of Wight. The period from 1861 to 1872, when she played a more normal role as Queen, was the most unpopular period of her reign. There were criticisms that the royal family was too expensive. Victoria did not carry out her public duties, lived out of London, and had a large family to support. Republicanism reached its highest point during this period, when the most important republicans were not extreme left-wingers but middle class Liberals. Disraeli's success in gaining the friendship and co-operation of the Queen was an important factor in winning power for the Conservatives at the end of the century. The monarchy was linked with the popularity of the Empire and Britain's greatness ✗.

Answer is incomplete. It needs more explanation of the years before 1837 and after 1902. Note the dates in the question.

Questions with model answers

A grade candidate – mark scored 8/10

For help: See Revise A2 Modern British and European History Study Guide pages 17–20

'All attempts at electoral reform between 1815 and 1914 were designed to preserve power for the few rather than extend it to the many.' *How accurate is this assessment of the motives behind political and electoral reform during this period?*

[WJEC question]

Examiner's Commentary

This claim is justified when assessing the motives of many of those who granted reform but is not a fair reflection of the motives of those who demanded change. The balance of power changed during this period. In 1815, those who resisted political and electoral change had control, reinforced by fears of the recent revolution in France. Change was seen as a threat to order. In 1914, the most important political battle was for women's suffrage; most men were entitled to vote ✔.

Good introduction that looks across the period.

During the nineteenth and early twentieth centuries, there were two consistent arguments against political reform: the existing system worked well and should not be changed for something which was unknown and probably dangerous, and the vote should be limited to property owners who had a stake in the country. Although the suffragette issue raised the particular problem of women's status, it also contained these two elements. `Power for the few' was intended but not in the autocratic sense which was seen in countries such as Russia.

The call for political reform continued throughout this period. The three major acts of 1832, 1867 and 1884 were preceded by demands for change that some tried to buy off by weak concessions and were followed by further demands for concessions, indicating that the quotation is correct. None of the measures completely satisfied the most determined radicals but they did enough to preserve the existing power structure. The aristocracy remained important politically, in the House of Lords and as ministers. Lord Rosebery was a Liberal Prime Minister at the end of the nineteenth century and Lord Salisbury was a Conservative Prime Minister at the beginning of the twentieth. Their two parties also dominated this period; the political changes did not bring the Labour party to power by 1914. Although the working classes gained the vote, they did not possess political power. The most considerable change was the growing influence of the industrial middle classes ✔.

Analytical approach that avoids narrative.

There were differences between the opponents of the successive reforms. The campaign for the 1832 Reform Bill was accompanied by riots that justified the fears of revolutionary outbreaks. However, the 1867 and 1884 acts were passed in a more peaceful manner. Disraeli's bill was introduced because he saw reform as both necessary and desirable if the Conservatives were going to win power but it was described as a `leap in the dark' because nobody was

A grade candidate continued

For help: See Revise A2 Modern British and European History Study Guide pages 17–20

Examiner's Commentary

sure of its consequences. It was a limited measure, intended to benefit the Tories, and has been described by Rubenstein as `a diabolically clever piece of Tory gerrymandering´ ✔.

Good quotation adds to the argument.

The 1884 Act extended the franchise but its effect can be exaggerated because a third of the men in England and Wales and a larger proportion in Scotland and Ireland could not vote. Both the Liberals and Conservatives supported it because they believed that it would benefit their parties.

Changes to the electoral system came later in the century. The abolition of the property qualification for MPs in 1858 did not immediately produce a new class of members and there were few working class MPs in 1914. The secret ballot was introduced in 1872 but corrupt elections were not prevented effectively until the 1880s and the two major political parties developed organisations that enabled them to hold on to power. Using such methods, the few retained power throughout this period ✔.

Conclusion widens the argument relevantly.

Exam practice questions

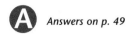

Answers on p. 49

(1) Why did Britain escape revolution during the period 1815–1918?

(2) **(a)** Explain the main changes introduced by the parliamentary reform Acts in

(i) 1832

(ii) 1867

(iii) 1884.

(b) Which of these reform Acts did most to encourage the development of democracy in the nineteenth century?

Answers

(1) **Key issue: The examination of an important development over an extended period.**

- Fears of a revolution at several points during this period, for example the 1820s before the Great Reform Act and Chartism in the 1840s. But never a real danger of the outbreak of a revolution. Continental revolutions as in 1830, 1848 and 1917 had little impact on Britain. General agreement about the British system, although particular grievances were widespread. Fears that these revolutions would spread to Britain were exaggerated.
- Governments used both repression and concession to control opposition. Protests against unemployment and high prices after 1815 were countered by the militia, legislation and more liberal policies in the 1830s. Police used against Chartists but petitions were allowed and Peel abolished the Corn Laws.
- Changes in the franchise and other electoral reform enabled more people to express their opinions legally. Politicians responsive to popular opinion. In the second half of the nineteenth century, Conservative and Liberal parties competed for popular support. Labour Party emerged by 1918 to represent working-class and trade union opinion.
- Governments' powers were more limited than in continental Europe. Parliaments were elected and met regularly. Newspapers reported freely and, although most were against radicalism, they allowed the expression of varied views.
- Trade unions were restricted but membership of trade unions was accepted by 1914. Contrasted with the prosecution of the Tolpuddle Martyrs in 1834. Extreme political groups attracted little support. Marxism had much less appeal than on the Continent. Socialism was democratic and peaceful rather than authoritarian and violent. Radical leaders were usually non-violent. Suffragettes became militant but did not call for a revolution. By 1918, the principle of women's suffrage was accepted.
- War caused revolutions in Europe. Napoleon III fell in 1870 because of the Franco-Prussian War. 1914–18 war caused revolutions in Russia and ended the monarchies in Germany and Austria-Hungary. However, although the war had serious effects on Britain, the government and the parliamentary system were not as unpopular.

(2) **Key issue: Explanation of the importance of parliamentary reform.**

(a) • 1832: Rotten or pocket boroughs were abolished. Some new boroughs (towns and cities) were given MPs. Franchise (votes) was given to borough householders with rates of at least £10. County franchise to £10 copyholders and £50 leaseholders and existing 50 shillings freeholders. These changes ended some of the previous unfairness in the distribution of seats. The franchise was widened to a limited extent.

Answers

- 1867: Borough franchise given to male householders and lodgers paying annual rent of £10. County franchise lowered to £12 copyholders. About 1,500,000 additional voters. Further redistribution of seats, e.g. Birmingham, Leeds, Liverpool, Manchester, and some extra MPs to growing counties.
- 1884: System of borough franchise extended to counties. Agricultural labourers received the franchise. Additional MPs given to large cities.

(b)
- 1832 was an important breakthrough. The first important change in the parliamentary franchise system and distribution of seats. However, comparatively few people received a vote. Changes affected the middle, not the working, class. Many growing boroughs still lacked MPs.
- 1867 was a major change because of the number of men who were given the vote for the first time. From this point, the working classes were a powerful influence in politics and governments had to respond to this pressure.
- 1884 completed the process of more votes for men and confirmed the importance of the working classes in Victorian politics.
- Each of the Acts was limited, although a strong claim can be made for either 1832 or 1867 as the most important. 1832 began the process but 1867 resulted in most additional votes. However, there were other limitations on the development of democracy that required reforms. Abolition of MPs' property qualification (1858), secret ballot (1872), the payment of MPs (not until 1911). Women lacked the vote throughout the nineteenth century.

Questions with model answers

C grade candidate – mark scored 6/10

 For help: See Revise A2 Modern British and European History Study Guide pages 40–42

Examine the changing problems faced by those who wished to expand the public education system during the period 1834–1945.

[OCR question]

Examiner's Commentary

Governments became more involved in education from the 1830s. In 1833, an annual grant of £20,000 was given to help to build the voluntary schools. Later the Privy Council was given some responsibility for spending the money and qualifications for teachers were introduced ✗.

This is relevant but highly narrative. Concentrate more on the key issue of problems in educational reform.

Inquiries in the middle of the century, such as the Newcastle Commission, led to more changes by investigating the different sorts of education that were available. It was clear that there was a need for more education and there were fears that Britain was falling behind other countries such as Germany and America. The Revised Code linked government grants to school results and proved unpopular. The 1870 Act showed how education was affected by the religious arguments. Governments were unwilling to take over the control of education whilst the religious groups argued over the balance between Church and nonconformist schools. The Act increased the number of schools and allowed Boards to pay the fees of poor children but there was still no compulsion about attendance and great dissimilarities in the amount and type of school provision. Compulsory attendance and higher age-leaving limits were introduced by the end of the century as universal education became more acceptable ✔.

Key developments in education with some explanation.

The twentieth century saw both gains and losses. Secondary and technical schools developed after the 1902 Act, when local authorities replaced school boards and children benefited from the introduction of medical inspections and some nursery schools ✗.

Why was the 1902 Act controversial? Some believed that government was intervening unnecessarily.

However, the depression led to a worsening situation. The government had to cut back on public spending and education was hit hard in the Geddes Axe. It was only when social reform became popular after the 1930s and during the Second World War that education was improved. Butler's Education Act of 1944 was supported by most of the country and the three major political parties. Although some thought that the measure went too far, they failed to prevent the introduction of major changes which included the creation of a Ministry of Education, reflecting the importance of education, the raising of the leaving age to 15, the end of fees for grammar schools which helped poor pupils and reorganisation into primary, secondary and further education ✔.

The answer deals with the period as a whole.

Questions with model answers

A grade candidate – mark scored 8/10

 For help: See Revise A2 Modern British and European History Study Guide pages 32–39

Why was state intervention adopted so slowly as the best means of tackling social problems in the nineteenth century?

Examiner's Commentary

Throughout much of the nineteenth century, the prevailing opinion of the large majority in the Conservative and Whig-Liberal parties was in favour of private responsibility and against state intervention in social issues. Like the economic arguments for laissez-faire, social problems were best solved by private initiative and self-reliance. State intervention would weaken the independence of the poor and would be an unreasonable burden on taxpayers. Even when state intervention was introduced, it was usually done to fill the gaps that the private sector could not fill. It was to be late in the nineteenth century when socialists pressed the principle of state intervention ✔.

Good introduction immediately focuses on the question.

The most powerful group in society in the century remained the great landowners, whose interests were against state intervention. In addition, the growing industrial and manufacturing middle class did not favour any limits by government on their activities. However, there was support for private charity, which was seen as a duty for the wealthy. This was thought to be a more moral means of helping the poor ✔.

Effective analysis of motives.

The reform of the Poor Law in 1834 came about because the existing system was thought to be inefficient and expensive although some believed that it would be too heavy a burden. It divided the nation between those whose taxes paid for the system and those who were reliant on the Poor Law and who continued to criticise the provisions.

There were many attempts by governments and other bodies to gather information about social problems. Select committees of Parliament and royal commissions investigated the Poor Law, charities, housing, factory conditions and the extent of disease. The census provided information. Factory acts were passed to prevent the employment of children and some women. Medical improvements were introduced late in the century. However, a common factor was that the legislation allowed but did not enforce reform, which depended on local initiatives. Inspectors were appointed whose reports provided further information but they had few powers.

The social reforms of Disraeli's ministry of 1874–80 might seem to prove that state intervention was accepted at this time. However, they were introduced partly because Gladstone's Liberals, who might seem to have supported reform strongly, had done little about the problems not because the Conservatives were enthusiastic about the principle. Measures such as the

A grade candidate continued

 For help: See Revise A2 Modern
British and European History
Study Guide pages 32–39

Examiner's Commentary

Public Health Act and the Artisans' Dwelling Act mostly drew together the different acts that had previously been passed. They usually gave powers to local authorities but did not guarantee that changes would take place.Disraeli's government, like others, was unwilling to risk the unpopularity of higher taxation. It can be argued that local schemes, such as Birmingham slum clearance under Chamberlain, were more effective than central plans ✔.

Factual knowledge supports the argument; no narrative.

This reluctance to support state intervention continued well into the twentieth century and was to be one of the major problems that Lloyd George faced when introducing his social reforms from 1908 to 1911. Only after the First World War and the depression of the 1930s was the principle fully accepted ✔.

Conclusion completes the argument effectively.

Exam practice questions

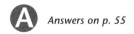

Answers on p. 55

Source-based questions: Old age-pensions, 1908

Read the following sources and then answer the questions which follow.

Source 1 *From a letter to* The Times *on the issue of pensions, July 1908*.

> However the Ministers may attempt to hide it, we are in fact in the presence of the universal out-door relief scheme divested of the restraining provisions of the present Poor Law. How can any prudent thinking man contemplate such a situation without dismay? The strength of this kingdom, in all its past struggles, has been its great reserve of wealth and the sturdy independent character of its people. The measure which is being pushed through the House of Commons with haste and acclaim will destroy both sources. It will extort wealth from its possessors by unjust taxation … It will distribute it in small doles, the most wasteful of all forms of expenditure, and will sap the character of the people by teaching them to rely, not on their own exertions, but on the State.

Source 2 *From a* Times *leader on the same issue, July 1908*.

> The bill is still widely and justifiably regarded as a leap in the dark which has not been accorded the measure of free discussion which is pre-eminently desirable. By their adoption of the non-contributory basis, the Government are undoubtedly defying the experience of many human generations in which the maxim has held good that free doles undermine the character, while thrift and providence sustain it. With non-contributory pensions and sixpenny football 'gates' the populace of a dozen years hence will nearly have [reached the point where they can have food and leisure without working for it].

(a) Study Sources 1 and 2.
To what extent do the sources agree in their criticisms of the proposed old-age pension scheme?

(b) Study both the sources and use your own knowledge.
Discuss the view that the Liberals had to deal with an extensive range of opposition, both from individuals and institutions, in order to pursue policies of social reform.

[AQA question]

Answers

Key issue: Assessment of a contemporary debate about old-age pensions.

Examiner's tip

Use only the sources to answer (a). Use the sources and your own knowledge to answer (b).

(a) • Significant that both sources are from *The Times*, the leading national newspaper. Most readers would probably have agreed with its criticism of the proposal to introduce old-age pensions. Source 1 is therefore typical of a wide body of opinion among its readers.

• Both sources accuse the government of pushing through the measure without enough discussion. Source 1 accuses ministers of hiding the truth of the scheme; Source 2 calls for more debate. These may be sincere claims but they might also be attempts merely to delay the legislation.

• Both sources use similar moral arguments – state intervention destroyed self-reliance. Source 1 strongly defends the existing Poor Law system, claiming that it made the poor independent. Supported indirectly by Source 2. Although it does not mention the existing Poor Law system, it contrasts the proposals unfavourably with 'the experience of many generations'.

• Source 1 includes an argument which is not used in 2, that the scheme would be an unfair tax on the wealthy and would be inefficient.

(b) • Source 2 represents opposition from an important institution, a leading newspaper. Writer of Source 1 is anonymous but was probably somebody who was wealthy, well educated and had a responsible job, like many others who opposed the pensions proposal.

• Conservatives opposed the measure. They could rely on the support of the House of Lords. Some Liberals opposed, supporting nineteenth-century laissez-faire against state intervention.

• Similar opposition to other social reforms of the Liberals after 1906, including national insurance and the People's Budget.

• Criticism of the Liberals came from employers, who objected to the expense and to less regulation of trade unions, and from some doctors who opposed national insurance.

• Criticism that social issues such as pensions were less important than defence and naval expenditure. Threat to the security of Britain and the Empire.

Questions with model answers

C grade candidate – mark scored 6/10

Which was more important to Britain in the period 1945 to 1963, Europe or the 'special relationship' with the USA? Explain your answer.

[AQA question]

There was not a `special relationship´ between Britain and the USA before the Second World War. Britain was more concerned with its empire and events in Europe whilst the USA was largely independent in its attitude to Britain and Europe. During the Second World War, they became close allies because of the common fight against Germany and Japan and the Cold War continued this `special relationship´. Policy towards Europe was more uncertain because British governments could not agree on the extent to which they should join the growing links between European countries ✔

The introduction is immediately relevant.

The relationship gave the USA an ally which supported it in most aspects of foreign policy as the struggle against communism continued. The British army was stationed in West Germany and elsewhere in the world whilst the navy was a powerful force. Britain benefited because it helped when Britain was a declining world power, withdrawing from many of its colonies. Some British politicians believed that Britain could use the `special relationship´ to act as a middleman between the USA and the USSR although these hopes were exaggerated.

Churchill, Macmillan and Thatcher saw themselves as the partners of Truman, Eisenhower and Reagan but their influence was exaggerated. As nuclear arms grew, it was too expensive for Britain to develop its own and it had to rely on the USA to supply weapons such as Polaris whilst Britain was a reliable European base for the USA.

The relationship was not always close. The USA did not support Britain over the Suez Crisis in 1956 and the Britain was unwilling to take part in the Vietnam campaign. However, the `special relationship´ resulted in military co-operation, during the Korean War of 1950-53 and the Gulf War of 1991. They usually had the same policies as members of the Security Council of the United Nations. The `special relationship´ can be exaggerated because both countries also had other interests but it was important to Conservative and Labour governments in Britain and to Democratic and Republican governments in the USA ✔.

Answer refers to the limits and extent of the key issue.

On the other hand, British policies to Europe changed. There was general agreement that Britain should co-operate with Europe but there were fears about European integration and some thought that this would harm the `special relationship´ with the USA. Therefore the `special relationship´ was more important ✗.

This is an example of an unbalanced answer. The answer is incomplete. There is not enough discussion of Europe as the question requires. You must answer all of the question.

A grade candidate – mark scored 8/10

For help: See Revise A2 Modern British and European History Study Guide pages 114–117 and 123–124

Why, in the twentieth century, has the Labour Party replaced the Liberals as the main opposition to the Conservatives?

At the beginning of the twentieth century, the Liberal Party was strong and from 1905 to 1914 formed a very effective government which carried through wide ranging reforms. Although the number of Liberal and Conservative MPs was similar after the 1910 election, the Liberals could rely on the support of the smaller Labour Party. By the end of the century, the numbers were reversed. The Labour Party challenged the Conservatives in power whilst there were few Liberal MPs. 4

Good introduction which discusses the question as a whole.

Social and political changes after the First World War harmed the Liberals and benefited the Labour Party. The Liberals lost some of their supporters from the business classes to the Conservatives whilst the working classes tended more to vote Labour. Although Lloyd George was a more successful wartime Prime Minister than Asquith, he was not forgiven for replacing the former Liberal Prime Minister and, after the war, he seemed closer to the Conservatives than to the Liberals. The number of Liberal MPs continued to fall and in the 1950s they had only 6 members ✔.

Important points can be made quickly.

More popular leaders such as Thorpe, Steel and Ashdown helped to revive the fortunes of the Liberals in the late twentieth century but they did not replace the Labour Party as the main opposition to the Conservatives.

The Labour Party increased its support among the industrial working classes and some of the middle classes. There was unity after their split in 1931 ✔.

Continues to analyse the key issue.

The Second World War was probably the most important reason for the rise of the Labour Party. It had a large majority after the 1945 election, attracting votes from most parts of the population. Since then, elections have resulted either in Labour or Conservative governments. Except in the early 1980s, the Labour Party avoided the splits that affected them when MacDonald was their leader in the 1930s and which helped to ruin the Liberals. They had a succession of able leaders. Attlee was quietly effective and was supported by talented ministers. Wilson appeared modern to the electorate and Callaghan was a skilful politician. Blair had a major personal impact at the end of the century. The party's policies were also brought up to date. After introducing the welfare state and nationalisation, Labour adapted to change and was able to present effective challenges to the Conservatives for much of the time. In defence and foreign policy, the policies were not very different from the Conservatives. The alliance with powerful trade unions was unpopular with the Conservatives but helped them to secure votes from the industrial classes ✔

Answer is balanced between the two parts of the question. This helps to get a high mark.

Exam practice questions

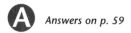

Answers on p. 59

(1) Analyse the factors that have promoted and hindered the participation of women in British democracy in the twentieth century.

(2) (a) What were most serious problems facing British Prime Ministers from 1945 to 1979?

(b) Who was the most successful British Prime Minister during the period from Attlee's election in 1945 to Callaghan's defeat in 1979?

Answers

(1)   Key issue: Analysis of the participation of women in democracy.

Examiner's tip

Avoid general statements about women. Examine both sides of the question.

- In 1918 women over 30 were given the vote, in 1928 vote at 21. Margaret Thatcher became the first female Prime Minister in 1979.
- The First World War was crucial in achieving the vote. Women had a wider variety of jobs. More in the Second World War in the women's services and as Land Girls and factory workers. Involved them more in public affairs, although the effects should not be exaggerated.
- More married women worked but did not have equal pay. Married women were debarred from some professional jobs. Changing family attitudes by the end of the century made it easier for middle-class women to lead independent lives. Gradual increase in public activities increased their involvement in democratic affairs. Educational opportunities increased with more women going to university. Primary-school teaching was particularly dependent on women.
- Feminist movement grew in the 1970s and brought about equal rights legislation. Political parties, especially Labour, became more sympathetic to women. In 1997, almost a quarter of Labour MPs were women, all middle-class.
- However, the total number of female MPs and ministers remained comparatively small. Constituencies were reluctant to select female candidates. Few women in the higher ranks of related employments, the civil service, law, universities, business and trade unions, from which many MPs were chosen. Women were more involved in local than national politics.

(2) (a)   Key issue: Explanation of major political problems.

Examiner's tip

Avoid narrative of 1945–79. Organise the problems in order of importance.

- Economic problems continued for much of the period. Second World War caused considerable damage to the economy. After the war, many factories were old with little investment in new techniques and machines. Growing competition from other countries, especially in the Third World, with cheaper labour. Traditional heavy industries (e.g. coal, steel, shipbuilding) and some more modern industries (e.g. cars) could not compete. Imports often exceeded exports.
- The welfare state was expensive (e.g. medical care, pensions, education). All parties supported universal provision but there were arguments about charges in medical care, level of pensions, standard of education. Amount of taxes was controversial: higher to maintain the welfare state or lower to encourage savings and private spending?
- Attitudes to foreign policy were largely agreed between the major parties: support for the American alliance and decolonisation. Problems over the level and types of defence. Left-wing Labour supporters opposed the reliance on nuclear weapons favoured by Labour and Conservative Prime Ministers. Different attitudes to European co-operation. Liberals were enthusiastic but remained small party. Labour and Conservative Prime Ministers faced problems in uniting their parties over the extent of co-operation with Europe.

Answers

- All parties avoided major divisions but Labour Prime Ministers were most affected. Attlee faced a split over health charges in 1951. Callaghan faced strong left-wing influence in Labour Party. Conservatives did not split but there were tensions and some ministers resigned over Suez (1956). Methods of Home's election as party leader and Prime Minister were unpopular with some Conservatives.

(b) Key issue: Comparison of Prime Ministers.

Examiner's tip

Focus on assessment of success and failure. Avoid description.

- Attlee: Prime Minister 1945–51. Success was that he was first Labour Prime Minister to govern with large majority (to 1950). Major reforms in National Health Service, nationalisation of industries. Began process of decolonisation. Good party manager with able men in his Cabinets. Failure was small majority (1950) and defeat (1951). Did not modernise the economy but this was probably impossible after the Second War in age of austerity.
- Churchill: Prime Minister 1951–55. Success was that he won power for Conservatives after heavy defeat in 1945. His ministry saw some economic revival. However, he remained best known as a former great war leader and contributed little to domestic issues. His personal achievements as peacetime Prime Minister were limited.
- Eden: Prime Minister 1955–57. Failures outweighed success as Prime Minister. Involved Britain in disastrous Suez Crisis. Failure and ill health led to resignation. Shortest premiership in this period.
- Macmillan: 1957–1963. Success was that he presided over extensive period of economic prosperity ('You never had it so good.'). Good relations with USA, Presidents Eisenhower and Kennedy. Mostly successful decolonisation. Modernised Conservative Party in spite of his own old-fashioned image. Failures included later economic problems. De Gaulle vetoed British application to join EEC. Scandals in ministry (e.g. Profumo Affair). Lost touch in later years.
- Home: Prime Minister 1963–64. Success was very limited. Regarded as honest in contrast to previous scandals. Conservatives lost 1964 election but by smaller margin than had been feared. Retained respect of Conservatives and others after defeat. Failures included the end of Conservative government. He compared badly with Wilson, the Labour leader.
- Wilson: Prime Minister 1964–70, 1974–76. Success included four election victories. Reputation as clever and up-to-date. Failures were that two governments had small majorities and first election of 1974 resulted in minority Labour government. Much time spent on saving government, not introducing policies of change. Balance-of-payment problems in 1970s. No agreement with trade unions over wages.
- Heath: Prime Minister 1970–1974. Success was that Britain joined the European Community. Failures were inflation, poor industrial relations, strikes, defeat after miners' strike. Troubles in Northern Ireland. Poor public image.
- Callaghan: Prime Minister 1976–79. Success, including holding together most of the Labour Party in spite of divisions over policy and breakaway of SDP. Recovery from severe economic problems. Failures included small majority, ending in minority government. Increasing strikes. 'Winter of discontent' (1978–79).

Questions with model answers

C grade candidate – mark scored 6/10

 For help: See Revise AS Modern British and European History Study Guide pages 51–53

Examiner's Commentary

Why did the Famine of 1845 have such impact on both Ireland and England?

The Famine was itself devastating to Ireland but it was also important in shaping political and economic developments in England. In Ireland, it had demographic, social, economic and political effects that changed the nature of Ireland and its relationship with England.

It is probable that about one million people died as a direct result of the Famine, about one eighth of the population, but the suffering contributed indirectly to other deaths. This decrease in population was unique in Europe. The emigration of more than two million people in the next fifteen years, which continued throughout the nineteenth century, also cut the population and created more bitterness against the British. This broke the pattern of previous years that had seen a rapid increase in the Irish population **✗**.

> This needs development. Ireland is a key issue.

The Famine had important effects in England because it was one of the most important reasons for the break-up of the Conservatives. They lost power for twenty years. It discredited Peel who had been one of the most effective prime ministers in the nineteenth century. He wished to conciliate Ireland although the Irish leaders such as O'Connell were closer to the Whigs. Peel wished to take a more moderate line and opposed the use of force. He tried to win the co-operation of the Roman Catholic Church and increased the grant to Maynooth College in spite of the unpopularity of the proposal among other English politicians, including the Conservatives. This was a small step but it showed a willingness to win over the Irish in an attempt to make them accept British rule **✔**.

> Good paragraph on Peel's aims towards Ireland.

Peel's hopes of further progress were dashed by the Famine because this affected the Corn Laws which were important to Conservative landlords and farmers. Arguments about free trade had continued since the early years of the century. Although cheap imports would help the industrial poor, the agricultural classes still dominated much of politics and there was a divide between Whig free trade and Conservative protectionism. Therefore, most Conservatives believed that policies should not change in spite of the famine problem in Ireland **✔**.

> Clear explanation of protectionism and free trade.

The repeal of the Corn Laws resulted in Peel's fall from power. He regarded it as his duty to bring in free trade to help the famine victims but fellow Conservatives regarded it as a betrayal of the party. No credit was given in Ireland because it was believed that the English Parliament had acted too late and only when forced to **✗**.

> The answer does not get a high mark because it is unbalanced on the two key issues.

Questions with model answers

A grade candidate – mark scored 8/10

For help: See Revise AS Modern British and European History Study Guide pages 46–51

'It was the role of key individuals which contributed most to the tensions which developed in Ireland between supporters and opponents of the Union during the period 1800–1900.' *For what reasons would you agree or disagree with this interpretation?*

[CCEA question]

Examiner's Commentary

The immediate cause of the union of 1800 was the need to ensure that Ireland would not weaken the war effort against France but it had been discussed previously but it was brought forward particularly because of the rebellion of 1798. It was hinted that Catholic Emancipation would be easier within a united kingdom whilst free trade would benefit the Irish community. By 1900, Catholic Emancipation had been achieved but the danger of rebellion remained and the Irish economy had not improved: the land issue was to be a particularly thorny issue. The divisions in Ireland between a politically dominant pro-Union Protestant governing class and anti-Union Catholics continued although the movement to repeal the Union attracted some Protestant support. Support in England for the Union united most people in the two major political parties until the end of the nineteenth century and defeated Gladstone's attempts to introduce Home Rule ✔.

Good introduction. Explains factors across the period.

The claim in the quotation that individuals contributed most to the tensions in Ireland is an exaggeration. Individuals had an important impact, pressing for or against the Union, but they reflected deeply held views. They accelerated or delayed developments but seldom directed them. Class interests, religion, the economic climate and British policy were fundamental factors in creating tensions ✔.

Discussion of the quotation deserves marks.

O'Connell's intervention was crucial in bringing about Catholic Emancipation but some English politicians had favoured this earlier in the century. The measure had most effect in England and his support for the Whigs in the 1830s lost his support in Ireland. The replacement of the moderate Isaac Butt by the more active Parnell marked a change in the Home Rule movement. Parnell was briefly successful in obstructing the business of the House of Commons and organising the boycott of unpopular landlords. A Protestant, he seemed able to win the support of both religions in Ireland. However, he did not unify the anti-Union movement in Ireland and he failed to benefit from the rivalries between Conservatives and Liberals. The intervention of Lord Randolph Churchill hardened pro-Union feeling in England and Ireland, especially in Ulster, but the response to his arguments showed that he did not create this opinion ✔.

Good analysis of some major figures.

A grade candidate continued

 For help: See Revise AS Modern British and European History Study Guide pages 46–51

Examiner's Commentary

The nationalist movement was also promoted by others whose activities demonstrated the variety of ways in which the Union was resisted. Charles Gavan Duffy's `The Vindicator´ and `The Nation´ and John Mitchel's militantly republican `United Irishman´ reflected the awareness of the importance of information and propaganda in newspapers. William Smith O´Brien, an example of a Protestant landowner who supported Catholic Emancipation, was involved in an unsuccessful rebellion in 1848. Such men added to the tensions at particular times but they were not major factors in the continuing tensions. They were symptoms rather than causes of the problem ✔.

Conclusion widens the argument relevantly.

Exam practice questions

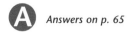 *Answers on p. 65*

Source-based questions: Rebellion in Ireland

Read the sources and answer the questions which follow.

Source 1   *Extract from a letter from General Lake, an Englishman who was in command of government forces in the province of Ulster, to Thomas Pelham, Chief Secretary, 25 March 1797.*

If we had a large body of troops in this district with martial law proclaimed, I think we should very shortly have all the arms in the country, and put an immediate stop to the rebellion. I see no other way of entirely disarming the province. It is not practicable without great force and such powers as I mention. The contagion spreads fast and requires most desperate remedies. I think if they knew that martial law was proclaimed and that one or two of their large towns were threatened to be burned unless arms were produced, it would have a great effect; and if they didn't, the houses of some of the disaffected should be set on fire.

You may think me too violent but I think it will be mercy in the end. I have patrols going every night and will do everything I can to thin the country of these rebellious scoundrels.

Source 2   *Extract from a letter from General Thomas Knox to General Lake, 18 March 1787. Knox was in command at Dungannon and his family were landowners in County Tyrone; he was MP for County Tyrone and controlled the corporation of Dungannon.*

In the counties of Down, Antrim, Derry and parts of Donegal and Tyrone, the whole population is hostile; consequently it should be the object of government to seize all their arms. But in the counties of Armagh, Cavan, Monaghan, Fermanagh, and the parts of Tyrone where my brigade is quartered, a portion of the people are hostile to the United Irishmen – calling themselves Orangemen. I have arranged to scour a district that is full of unregistered arms. I do not hope to succeed to any great extent but I hope to increase the animosity between the Orangemen and the United Irishmen. Upon that animosity depends the safety of the centre counties of the North. Were the Orangemen disarmed or put down, the whole of Ulster would be as bad as Down or Antrim.

(a)   Consult Sources 1 and 2. Explain and compare their views on the role of the army in putting down rebellion.

(b)   Using the sources and your own knowledge, would you agree that the counter-insurgency policies provoked a premature, and therefore unsuccessful rebellion?

[CCEA question adapted]

Answers

Key issue: Comparison of primary sources.

Examiner's tip

(a) – Note similarities and differences in the sources. (b) – You must use both the sources and your own knowledge.

(a) • Sources agree that the situation was serious. Danger that rebellion would spread throughout Ulster. Both writers believed that disarmament was necessary. Sources were written at the same time but authors had different backgrounds. Lake: English army general. Knox: General and also an important Irish landowner and MP. Probable that Knox was better informed about the situation. Lake generalised the extent of the unrest. Knox points out that, whilst some provinces were rebellious, others were less anti-British.

   • Solutions in the sources are different. Source 1 wants a completely military solution with the enforced disarmament of all of Ulster. Lake would not only impose complete martial law but would make an example of the ringleaders by violent means. Source 2 prefers a more political approach. Also wishes to arm the Unionists (Orangemen) against the rebels.

(b) • Sources show that, although Lake and Knox differed in their solutions, both believed that there was a considerable danger of rebellion. Lake would deal with it immediately by extreme military methods. Knox favoured a more subtle approach, dividing the Irish by encouraging the hostility between Orangemen and United Irishmen.

   • Fears of a French invasion. 1797 armada to Fishguard was unsuccessful but government feared a more determined attempt on Ireland. Naval battle of Camperdown ended the danger.

   • Former Presbyterian moderates in Ulster gave way to more violent agitators. Lord-lieutenant Camden resorted to strong measures which involved using local yeomanry. Result was virtual civil war. Fearing suppression, the United Irishmen decided to act. Lacked organisation, arms and French help. Open risings were put down by the military. Remaining resistance was suppressed by terror.

   • Premature? This indicates that a later, better-planned rising would have succeeded. Rebels would probably never have sufficient arms, although a more organised rising would probably have been more dangerous and longer lasting.

Questions with model answers

C grade candidate – mark scored 6/10

 For help: See Revise A2 Modern British and European History Stud Guide pages 78 and 130–131

Why did the Bolsheviks, rather than more Liberal Democrats, gain power by the end of 1917?

Examiner's Commentary

The Revolution broke out in 1917 because the Russians had become disillusioned with the rule of Nicholas II. The war resulted in food shortages, heavy casualties and defeats by Germany. Nicholas II's war leadership made him personally unpopular and the government was discredited by the unpopularity of the Tsarina and the corruption of Rasputin ✔.

Satisfactory survey of the background of the revolution.

When there were strikes and riots in St. Petersburg, the soldiers did not support the Tsar but sympathised with the rioters. Nicholas II was soon persuaded to abdicate and a provisional government was set up under Lvov. Germany allowed Lenin to return to Russia in a sealed train but an attempt by the Bolsheviks to seize power failed and Lenin had to flee. Kerensky became Prime Minister but he made the mistake of trying to continue the war against Germany, which made his government very unpopular ✗.

Factually accurate but is narrative. Needs more explanation and analysis.

The worsening conditions in Russia enabled the Bolsheviks to carry out another revolution against Kerensky. The Winter Palace, the centre of government, was stormed and Lenin claimed that the Congress of Soviets, with communist commissars, had supreme power. The Bolsheviks soon took over control of the most important cities and factories. By the end of 1917, the communists were in power ✗.

Again – accurate but highly narrative. More analysis of the Bolshevik success would get a higher mark.

The Bolsheviks had several advantages over the liberal democrats. Lenin was a more able leader than Kerensky and was ruthless enough to seize power and to ignore the existing government. Although the Bolsheviks were a minority, they overcame this disadvantage by seizing the most important centres of power. They soon made sure that they controlled the army and police. Lenin's slogan of 'Peace, Land and Bread' was more popular than Kerensky's programme because it reflected what most people wanted. Peace meant an end to an unpopular war, land was promised to the serfs whilst bread was needed to end the famine which resulted from the war ✔.

Paragraph includes explanation and is the best part of the answer.

A grade candidate – mark scored 8/10

For help: See Revise AS Modern British and European History Study Guide pages 75–77

'Faced by major political and economic problems the tsarist regime was unable to adapt in response to revolutionary pressure.' *How valid is this assessment of Russia between 1815 and 1917?*

[WJEC question]

Examiner's Commentary

The Tsarist regime was very successful until the beginning of the twentieth century in withstanding revolutionary pressures and it seemed stable even in 1914. The First World War was more effective in bringing about revolution than all of the previous pressures. The Romanovs were the most powerful and the last absolute monarchs in Europe and were able to resist the challenges to change almost until the time of their fall. Although they did not adapt to revolutionary pressure, they were able to survive and retain most of their power ✔.

Interesting introduction, which challenges the quotation.

There were demands for political change from the reign of Nicholas I, who had to suppress the Decembrist revolt in 1825. Alexander II's emancipation of the serfs and introduction of the zemstvos led to calls for more political changes whilst his later reactionary period encouraged extremists such as the Nihilists. However, his assassination in 1881 led to the firm autocracy of Alexander III. The most serious revolutionary challenge before 1914 was the 1905 Revolution but its outcome showed the weakness of the revolutionaries and the strength of Nicholas II's regime ✔

Avoids unnecessary narrative. High marks are given for clear but brief arguments.

The Romanovs could rely on the army and police, for example in the 1905 Revolution. They were also supported by the landowning aristocracy, whose grievances were less important than their common interests with the tsars against revolutionaries. The Orthodox Church was a powerful ally and the government used extreme censorship for most of this period. Many Russians regarded the tsar as the 'father' of the nation and their absolute power meant that the only alternative seemed to be extreme revolution. 'Russification' meant that most Russians believed themselves to be different from other European countries and they did not favour the introduction of western models of government. The tsars were fortunate because the opposition was usually disorganised and divided. It was only in 1917 that they were faced by an organised and well-supported opposition.

The Romanovs were less successful in dealing with economic changes. Nicholas I recognised the problem of serfdom and the backwardness of Russian agriculture but did nothing important to deal with the problem. Alexander II's emancipation of the serfs resulted in a slight increase in production but did not improve agriculture very much. Industry improved at the end of the nineteenth century, the railway system grew and Russia had

Questions with model answers

A grade candidate continued

 For help: See Revise A2 Modern British and European History Study Guide pages 75–77

Examiner's Commentary

plenty of raw materials but the middle class was weak and there was little investment from within Russia. Witte's policies to encourage industry were successful in the short term. Production increased but it resulted in problems as well as benefits. The large numbers who crowded into the towns could become discontented and were a target for revolutionaries. Riots became more common and the pressures were a major cause of revolution in 1917 ✔.

Balanced argument (political and economic problems) gets a high mark.

None of the tsars from 1815 to 1917 seriously considered the need for change. Concessions were limited and given reluctantly. The usual policy was repression. However, to 1914 it seemed as if this policy could work. The October Manifesto gave some political concessions and the economy seemed stable. However, the regime's weakness and inability to adapt was shown when Russia was involved in the disastrous First World War ✔.

Conclusion does not repeat points that have been made previously.

Exam practice questions

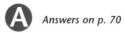 *Answers on p. 70*

(1) Consider the arguments for and against the claim that Russia was the most serious threat to European peace from 1815 to 1914.

(2) (a) Explain the problem of serfdom in Russia from 1815 to 1917.

(b) How did the tsars try to deal with the problems caused by serfdom during this period?

Answers

(1)   **Key issue: Assessment of Russia's international role.**

Examiner's tip

'Most dangerous' means that you must compare Russia with other countries.

- Russia: Crimean War (1854–56) was the most extensive war in nineteenth century. Russia had a major responsibility because of its ambitions against Turkey. Russia usually followed a policy of nationalism and orthodoxy. Champion of the Slavs and the Orthodox Church. Constant issue in the Eastern Question which continued throughout this period. Russia made enemies of every other European country during this period; its alliances tended to be temporary. Turkey was the enemy. Austria was a rival in the Balkans. Britain and France were hostile during much of the nineteenth century. Germany was an enemy by 1914; the alliance made with Bismarck was short-lived. Russia was not responsible for the Sarajevo crisis but its support for Serbia and its mobilisation were crucial to the outbreak of war in 1914.
- Austria: Metternich system tried to maintain international peace after 1815. War was dangerous to Austria. Austria's commitment to the Balkans and eastern Europe caused instability. Austrian reaction in the Sarajevo crisis was a direct cause of the 1914 war.
- Germany: Prussia before Bismarck was a weak international power but Bismarck unified Germany through war against Denmark, Austria and France. Policy which continued under William II. Determined that Germany should become a world power and deliberately challenged Britain's naval power.
- France: France was the major international threat in 1815 but played a less active role to 1848. Napoleon III's Third Empire was involved in several crises but was less dangerous to peace than Prussia. From 1871, the French desire for revenge was a constant source of instability but France was less dangerous than Germany and the Balkans crises.

(2)   **Key issue: Explanation of problem of Russian serfdom.**

Examiner's tip

Note the period in the question. A high mark requires a broad range.

(a) • 80% of Russians were serfs. Added to landlords, the vast majority of Russians were linked to serfdom.
- Serfdom gave nobles considerable power. Could sell serfs, force army service, give legal punishments, exile to Siberia.
- Social unrest. Rebellions against landlords because serfs had no other means of expression.
- Inefficient economic system. Serfs had no incentive to improve production or adopt new methods. Lack of labour for new industries.
- Affected military efficiency. Unwilling serf conscripts led to failure in Crimean War.

(b) • Alexander I did not change the serf system. Nicholas I recognised need for change, especially with rebellions, but minor reforms achieved little. Police, army and censorship used to suppress troublemakers.

- Alexander II issued edict of emancipation (1861). Serfs were personally free but landlords retained land. Serfs had to buy land with down payment of 20% and rest over 49 years with interest. Mirs (village communities) handled property ownership, collecting redemption payments and distributing land.
- Many serfs could not afford to buy land. Became landless and moved to towns. Others in debt. Best land usually kept by landlords. Many serfs then controlled by unpopular mirs.
- Emancipation did not lead to the modernisation of Russian economy. Landlords used money to pay off debts, not invest in industry.
- Alexander III was repressive and uninterested in reform. Nicholas II also reactionary until 1905 Revolution. Then allowed Stolypin to introduce moderate reforms, including encouragement of kulaks, more prosperous farmers, who would support regime. Only 15% of peasants were kulaks by 1914. In spite of repression and living conditions, most peasants were still loyal to Nicholas in 1914. Hardship in First World War created a demand for land and bread, which was promised by Lenin. Serfs became part of the revolutionary forces.

Questions with model answers

 For help: See Revise A2 Modern British and European History Stu Guide pages 93–94 and 132–136

C grade candidate – mark scored 6/10

Examiner's Commentary

Were economic factors more than important than ideology in the development of Russian foreign policy during the period 1917–2000?

[CCEA question adapted]

After gaining power, the Russian communists did not pursue an active foreign policy. The Whites in the civil war were supported by foreign troops, including French and British soldiers. Russia did not take part in the post-war conferences because of the civil war and because it had already signed the Treaty of Brest-Litovsk with Germany. Lenin then concentrated on strengthening Bolshevik power within Russia rather than embarking on an active and expensive foreign policy. Thus economic factors were more important than the ideology of spreading communism, in spite of Trotsky's programme of world revolution. Stalin pursued the policy of `socialism in one country´, partly for economic reasons and partly because, like Lenin, he wished to reorganise Russia internally. Russia did not become a member of the League of Nations until 1934 and did not then play an important part in its work ✔.

Satisfactory explanation of foreign policy to 1934.

Stalin signed a Pact with Hitler (1939) but this did not prevent the invasion of Russia in 1941. At first, the German army was very successful and the Russians had to withdraw. The cold climate, poor supplies and the large number of Russian reinforcements meant that the tide turned against the Germans. After suffering heavy losses, the German army was defeated at Stalingrad and Leningrad. The battle of Kursk was the largest tank battle in the war and made victory certain for Russia. Russian troops then advanced to Berlin and Russia took control of Eastern Europe ✗.

This section is unnecessary. It is an account of the war, not a study of foreign policy.

Ideology affected Stalin's policies in the Cold War to some extent. One reason why he rejected American aid to Russia and its allies was because he was anti-capitalist. However, economic and political motives were more important. Millions of Russians were killed in the Second World War and industry had been ruined. Surviving German factories under Russian control were stripped and their machinery was sent to Russia. Eastern European countries were expected to assist the Russian economy. Comecon was set up (1949) to organise trade between Russia and its allies and Yugoslavia was expelled when it refused to co-operate ✔.

Good comparison of ideology and economy.

For help: See Revise A2 Modern British and European History Study Guide pages 79–83

C grade candidate continued

Examiner's Commentary

Political and military reasons were important in Russian policy after the Second World War. Russia soon took political control of countries such as East Germany, Poland, Hungary and Czechoslovakia and they became communist states. Historians disagree how far Stalin tried to expand into the rest of Europe but the Cold War resulted in hostility between east and west. The Berlin Blockade (1948-49) showed how far Stalin would go to impose Russian power in Russia ✔.

Paragraph considers an alternative explanation.

Therefore, although ideology was a continuing factor in Russian foreign policy, it was less important than economic and political issues ✗.

The answer is incomplete. The question ends in 2000 but the answer does not mention the post-Stalin period. Pay attention to any dates given in the question.

A grade candidate – mark scored 8/10

Consider the arguments for and against the claim that Stalin depended on the dictatorship already established by Lenin.

[OCR question]

Stalin claimed to be Lenin's heir when he came to power in 1924 and Lenin remained a public hero during Stalin's rule. However, historians disagree about the extent to which there was continuity between Lenin's and Stalin's governments. Some see Lenin as beginning the process of dictatorship and state control that was continued by Stalin whilst others believe that Stalin's state was very different ✔.

Interesting introduction' which offers two alternative explanations.

Stalin rose to power under Lenin, being editor of 'Pravda' and becoming a Commissar. He was active during the civil war and then became general secretary of the central committee of the communist party. This gave him considerable power and won him the support of other important party leaders such as Kamenev and Zinoviev. His rise to power would not have been possible without Lenin's approval ✔.

Lenin made Russia a one-party state but had to come to terms with pressures that led to the introduction of the NEP. Non-party people could make a contribution to the state and could hold local offices. Differences were even tolerated within the Bolsheviks. For example, Bukharin was more moderate than Trotsky. At first, Stalin sided with the moderates, supporting 'socialism in one country' against Trotsky's more revolutionary programme. However, when he was firmly in power, Stalin suppressed ruthlessly anybody who had different views. Former allies such as Bukharin were killed during the purges. Trotsky had been a respected leader under Lenin but was driven out and then murdered by Stalin.

Relevant account of Stalin's rise.

Questions with model answers

A grade candidate continued

 For help: See Revise A2 Modern British and European History Study Guide pages 79–83

Examiner's Commentary

Whilst Lenin had seen the Bolsheviks as a minority who would direct Russia until all of the country adopted their views, Stalin was determined to force his policies on all Russians. The liquidation of the independent kulaks was a political as well as an economic policy. At the same time, Lenin's personal role was different from Stalin. Although Lenin was the hero of the revolution and the founder of the communist state, he remained less concerned about the details of policy. Stalin's personal power and his use of propaganda meant that he was a more powerful master of the state ✔.

Comparative approach gets a high mark.

However, one must not underestimate Lenin's ruthlessness although his methods might have been different. The secret police and the army continued to suppress opposition as in tsarist Russia but the scale of his persecution was less than Stalin's. In 1917, it was Lenin's daring and skill that won power for the Bolsheviks whilst his willingness to adapt after 1917 was designed to keep power, not to share it. Stalin's dictatorship was more extreme and more personal but it was essentially similar. In spite of their differences, there was an underlying continuity between the totalitarian governments of Lenin and Stalin ✔.

Conclusion has a clear judgement about the question.

Exam practice questions

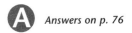 *Answers on p. 76*

(1) Why was there no effective resistance to the communist regime within the USSR from 1917 to 1964?

(2) (a) Compare the effects of the First and Second World Wars on Russia.

(b) Why was Russia more successful in the Second World War than in the First?

Answers

(1)   Key issue: The internal opposition to Soviet governments.

Examiner's tip

An analytical essay will be worth higher marks than a narrative answer.

- Communist system was totalitarian, with full control of political, economic and social systems. All the agencies of state crushed opposition and, from the 1930s, no alternative views within the communist party.
- No aspect of life outside state control. Everybody had to follow the party line and, from 1929, especially Stalin's line, including the arts and media, education and religion. Secret police were widespread. Purges and political commissars controlled the army. Purge of the kulaks and the treatment of racial minorities showed the extent of Stalin's willingness to impose his policies.
- Class structure prevented an organised opposition. No westernised middle class or free working class.
- Communism claimed to represent a proletarian revolution and a people's democracy. Universal suffrage but in practice a small group in the party held power. Lenin then Stalin dominated government. Propaganda promoted their importance. Stalin especially purged real and imagined rivals in government and potential enemies in the military, professional and industrial classes.
- Criticism of the regime was denounced: capitalist, anti-revolutionary and unpatriotic, Trotskyists or Fascists. Lenin was seen as the hero of the Revolution; Stalin was portrayed as the saviour in the Second World (Great Patriotic) War against Nazi Germany.

(2)   Key issue: Assessment of two major wars on Russia.

Examiner's tip

(a) and (b) require comparisons. Avoid sequential narratives.

(a)
- Both wars caused economic hardships. Harvests were affected in First World War because of number of men needed for army. Railways could not distribute enough food. Large areas of Russian land were overrun in Second World War. Industries destroyed.
- Russia's armies were weak at beginning of both wars. In 1914 and 1941, the army was badly equipped and had no clear war plans. Officers were inefficient but for different reasons. 1914 Russian officers badly trained. Stalin's purges in the 1930s weakened the officer class; replaced by inexperienced officers who were afraid to take initiatives.
- First World War caused a revolution by exposing the inefficiency of the tsarist government and Nicholas II's weakness as a military leader. Communist regime enforced obedience in Second World War. Political commissars ensured obedience to the party. Stalin's early mistakes were concealed and he became the heroic leader, responsible for delivering victory. War strengthened Stalin's position.

(b) • First and Second World Wars began similarly with heavy defeats. Battle of Tannenburg (1914). Rapid German advance as far as Leningrad, Stalingrad and almost Moscow by 1942. Russian army had inferior weapons and was badly led.

• Russia in First World War was unable to recover from defeat. Superior manpower and resources in Second World War (and German mistakes) brought victory.

• The tsarist government could not reorganise an effective war effort. Stalin's government used ruthless methods to hold up the German advance and then gain victory.

• Nicholas II did not receive effective assistance from allies. Gallipolli attack failed (1915). Stalin received aid from USA and Britain that helped to support the Russian war effort. In spite of differences, the anti-German alliance was more effective in Second World War than in the First.

Questions with model answers

C grade candidate – mark scored 6/10

 For help: See Revise A2 Modern British and European History Study Guide pages 55–61

'Germany was made by its economy.' *How valid is this view of Germany from 1815 to 1900?*

Examiner's Commentary

Keynes said that German unification depended more on `coal and iron than on blood and iron´ and the German economy was very successful in the nineteenth century ✔.

Useful quotation but it should be explained.

The Zollverein was an agreement between German states to trade freely with each other. Prussia was the leader and other states included Bavaria, Hanover and Saxony. Although large parts such as Hamburg stayed outside, most German states joined by 1840 and the abolition of customs duties improved their economies.

Railways expanded more in Germany than in other European countries and were centred on Prussia. This allowed goods to be transported more quickly and in larger volumes and encouraged German exports to the rest of Europe, Britain and overseas. The German economy was strong at the end of the nineteenth century. The Ruhr, the Saar and Alsace-Lorraine contained many raw materials. There were large banks which encouraged investment in industry and towns grew when people moved from the countryside for employment. Many peoples migrated to Germany from other parts of Europe to seek jobs. There was expansion in coal, iron and steel and large companies such as Krupps developed. Germany also had new industries such as electrical and chemical firms. As a result, exports increased and the German navy grew ✔.

Relevant discussion of different parts of the German economy.

Germany produced dynamos, sulphuric acid, dyes, fertilisers, explosives and arms. German cities and factories could use electricity more than in any other European country. Germany´s merchant navy was larger than any other continental country and only second to Britain´s ✗.

Repeats the points in the previous paragraph.

Therefore, Germany became the most prosperous country in Europe with a modern economy. It contrasted with the backward economy of Russia and even France. ✗

A weak conclusion. The answer is very descriptive and incomplete. It does not discuss whether 'Germany was made by its economy'.

A grade candidate – mark scored 8/10

For help: See Revise A2 Modern British and European History Study Guide pages 55–61

How far do you agree that Prussianism was more important than nationalism in Germany from 1815 to 1914?

Examiner's Commentary

The German Confederation or Bund was set up in the Vienna settlement under the leadership of Austria. The Bund was a loose form of German unity and there was a German culture, especially in drama, music and poetry. However, there was little feeling of German political nationalism. There were differences between the different states, some of which were Protestant whilst others were Catholic. States such as Prussia were industrialising but others were more traditionally agricultural. Many non-Germans lived within the territories of the Bund and Germans lived outside in other states, especially in Austria. The result was that there were alternative views of unification. Some preferred greater Germany (Grossdeutschland), a federal state which would include Austria, and others wished for a smaller Germany (Kleindeutschland) which would exclude Austria ✔.

Good analysis of the basic issues in German nationalism at the beginning of the period.

Prussia was the leading German state within the Bund although it was not as strong as Austria. The Zollverein (1834) gave Prussia economic leadership among German states, especially when Austria was excluded. The problems of German nationalism were clear in the 1848 Revolution when the Frankfurt Parliament aimed at a Kleindeutschland but depended on Prussia to lead the movement. Frederick William IV refused to accept the crown of a united Germany and helped to put down the Revolution. The Olmütz Convention (1850) was a setback to German nationalism because it restored Austria's leadership in Germany ✔.

Clear reasons why Prussia was important in Germany.

Bismarck's unification of Germany in the 1860s depended more on Prussian strength than on German nationalism. He was a conservative junker rather than a liberal nationalist and he criticised the `speeches and majority verdicts' of the 1848 revolutionaries. His aim was to promote Prussian interests and he probably wanted first to unify the northern states under Prussia rather than unify all of Germany. The constitution of the new German Empire gave most power to Prussia. The King became Kaiser or Emperor with extensive powers. Bismarck was Chancellor, Minister-President and Foreign Minister and it was expected that future Chancellors and most ministers would be Prussian. Prussia had most members of the powerful Bundesrat whilst the Reichstag, which was more widely elected, was less important ✔.

Good analysis of Prussia and nationalism in the 1860s. Avoids narrative.

In foreign policy, William II wished to expand German power and the appeal of this Prussianist feeling won him support from the army and from the general public. There was also increasing hostility to international movements such as socialism and to non-German groups such as the Jews. Prussianism, was the driving force in Germany and determined policy whilst the liberal nationalists and the interests of other German states were unimportant ✔.

Good understanding of the whole of the period. Always relevant.

Exam practice questions

 *Answers on p. 81*

(1) 'William II did not depart from the foreign policy which Bismarck pursued after 1871. He only pushed it to its logical conclusion.' *Consider the arguments for and against this claim.*

(2) **(a)** How consistent were Bismarck's aims from 1862 to 1871?

(b) Why was Bismarck more successful in uniting Germany than the revolutionaries of 1848–49?

Answers

(1)   **Key issue: Comparison of the foreign policies of Bismarck and William II.**

Examiner's tip

Avoid sequential narratives in comparative questions. The question requires you to consider aspects for and against the quotation.

Arguments for the claim:

- Bismarck's aim was to defend German interests. Used diplomacy and interpreted international developments within this aim. This was also William's sole aim and his view of international developments.
- Policies led to the hostility of France, especially because of the take over of Alsace-Lorraine. Franco-German relations were a major source of instability until 1914. Bismarck tried to isolate France by winning the friendship of the other major Continental countries, Austria-Hungary and Russia. William II never attempted to conciliate France.
- Attempts to build a secure alliance system could not work permanently because Austria-Hungary and Russia had opposing interests in the Balkans. The Dual Alliance (1879) with Austria-Hungary excluded Russia. The Dreikaiserbund and Reinsurance Treaty (1887) failed. William II strengthened the Austrian alliance, pushing Russia into an alliance with France and later Britain.

Arguments against the claim:

- Bismarck believed in diplomacy and wished to avoid another war. William II was willing to risk war at several points and German policy was largely responsible for war in 1914. Bismarck thought that Germany was a 'satiated' (satisfied) country after 1871: he did not want to expand German territory further. William II pursued expansionist policies.
- Bismarck did not believe in the value of colonies and embarked reluctantly on colonisation. William II was enthusiastic about developing German influence abroad, for example his friendship with Turkey, the Kruger Telegram, the Morocco crises.
- Bismarck wanted to retain Britain's friendship and did not favour Germany strengthening its navy, which would threaten Britain's vital interests. William II was keen to make Germany a world naval power, a direct challenge to Britain, which joined the Triple Entente.

(2)   **Key issue: Assessment of Bismarck's aims.**

Examiner's tip

Focus on consistency: how far did Bismarck change? Question is about aims – avoid narrative.

(a) • Historians have suggested two alternative explanations: (1) Bismarck always wished to unify all of Germany, (2) Bismarck initially wanted to unify only north Germany and changed his mind later. Many historians now support the second view.

- Bismarck was consistent in putting Prussia first. The test was always whether policies and events would benefit Prussia, not Germany.
- His aim was to ensure the power of the King and the junkers; he opposed the Liberals.

Answers

- His aims remained realistic. He never confronted a strong enemy and sought either to win allies against an enemy (e.g. Austria against Denmark) or to ensure neutrality (e.g. France against Austria).
- Bismarck probably believed that the unification of Germany would take place some time but did not plan it in 1866. He was doubtful about the value of southern, Catholic German states. France was as responsible as Prussia for the 1870 war. This represented a change in his immediate aims.

(b)
- 1848–49 revolutionaries lacked clear aims: small Germany (Kleindeutschland) or large Germany (Grossdeutschland)? Bismarck's aims were clearer. To replace Austrian power by Prussia in Germany. Nobody similar to Bismarck in 1848–49 to provide firm leadership.
- 1848–49 dominated by Liberals who had little support. Bismarck preferred 'blood and iron' to 'speeches and majority votes'. Bismarck ignored the liberals in the Landtag (lower House of Parliament) to raise money for the army.
- 1848–49 lacked military power. Bismarck used the army and relied on Roon and Moltke. Prussian army modernised. By 1870 the army had defeated Austria and France, two other major powers.
- 1848–49 Prussia withdrew support from the revolution. Frederick William IV refused offer of German crown from the Frankfurt Parliament. During 1860s, William I supported Bismarck, sometimes reluctantly.
- 1870–71 Bismarck could force all German states to join new empire; impossible in 1848–49.

Questions with model answers

C grade candidate – mark scored 6/10

Contrast Germany's relations with France after the First and Second World Wars.

The bitterness between Germany and France was intense in 1918. Hostility between the countries was a major cause of the First World War and much of the fighting took place on the frontiers between them. Memories of the French defeat in 1870 and the Alsace Lorraine issue caused deep divisions. The balance of power was different in 1918 because France was now the victor. The scale of Germany's defeat and France's desire for revenge shaped the relations between the two countries until the outbreak of the Second World War ✔.

> *Clear explanation of the situation in 1918. Good introductions help to get high marks.*

Germany had to give many concessions to France in the Treaty of Versailles. Alsace Lorraine was returned. France occupied the rich Saar region and the Rhineland between Germany was demilitarised. The heaviest burden was the reparations which Germany had to pay, mostly to France. France insisted on full payment although Germany could not afford it and occupied the Ruhr in 1923 when Germany did not fulfil its quota ✔.

> *Sound analysis of Versailles.*

In the 1930s France followed a policy of appeasement to Hitler. Germany did not threaten France directly but Hitler used appeasement to expand German territories, for example in Czechoslovakia. He believed correctly that French politicians would follow Britain's lead and would not act independently against Germany ✗.

> *No link with the previous part of the answer. Answers should develop clearly.*

Daladier, the French Prime Minister, was at Munich but he played a less important part than Chamberlain when the Sudetenland was handed over to Germany. France also followed Britain's lead in declaring war when Poland was invaded in 1939. Germany's swift victory over France in 1940 showed how the balance of military power had changed again.

Although Germany was defeated again in the Second World War, relations with France were very different from 1918. Germany did not have to pay reparations and did not surrender any territory. Within a few years, West Germany and France were partners in the European Coal and Steel Community which laid the foundations of the European Community and later European Union. The countries also became military allies ✗.

> *Why did relations change? More explanation needed for high mark. The answer begins well but is uneven.*

Questions with model answers

A grade candidate – mark scored 8/10

For help: See Revise A2 Modern British and European History Study Guide pages 141–146

Why did fascism appeal more than liberalism to Germany in the inter-war period?

Examiner's Commentary

Many Germans were disillusioned during the Weimar Republic. It was founded after Germany was defeated in the First World War and never recovered from the fact that it had to accept the Versailles settlement. By 1933, Hitler and the Nazis set up a fascist government which survived until 1945. However, the Germans were probably attracted as much by Hitler's practical policies as they were by the ideas of fascism ✔.

Introduction discusses the key issue of fascism and liberalism. No vague background.

The liberalism of the Weimar Republic was shown by its system of government. The President was elected for a limited period although he was allowed emergency powers in an emergency. Proportional representation meant that minority political parties could be represented in the Reichstag. A federal system which gave some powers to the regions meant that the government was decentralised. However, the tolerant liberal system allowed extreme parties to grow and there were violent uprisings by communist Spartacists and right-wing Nazis. The army officer class remained influential in spite of the defeat in the First World War, which was blamed more on politicians than on the military, and Field Marshal Hindenburg became the respected second President of the Republic.

The economic problems of the 1920s affected everybody in Germany. Although there was some improvement during the Stresemann era when foreign investment increased and Germany's reparations were eased by the Dawes and Young Plans, the Wall Street Crash of 1929 plunged the economy into turmoil again. The Weimar Republic was blamed for the problems although it was not responsible for the heavy reparations and the damage which resulted from the First World War. The Germans believed that liberal economic policies did not work ✔.

Sound analysis of the weakness of political and economic liberalism.

Fascism was supported in Germany, as in Italy and Spain, because it promised to restore political and economic order. Hitler would be a powerful leader who was dedicated to serving his country instead of the failed politicians of Weimar who were considered to be corrupt. The single Nazi party was a contrast to the weak coalition governments which ruled Germany immediately after the First World War and would protect the German business classes from communism ✔.

Contrasts Weimar and the Nazis. Good point made briefly gets high marks.

A grade candidate continued

*For help: See Revise A2 Modern
British and European History
Study Guide pages 141–146*

Examiner's Commentary

Hitler took advantage of people's fears to gain and hold power. The Reichstag Fire was blamed on the communists and the Enabling Law allowed him to set up a dictatorship in a one-party state. His popularity was shown when 96% of people voted for him in a plebiscite. As Führer, he was head of the state and received a personal oath of loyalty from army officers. His nationalism and determination to regain the losses which Germany had suffered at Versailles won him the support both of the officer class and of the general public. It was claimed that Jews were a danger to racial purity and the German economy, creating unemployment and acting as greedy money-lenders. Nazi economic policies concentrated on public works which created employment. Although the success of these policies was more limited than the Nazis claimed, the stability of the currency was restored and living standards rose after the 1920s.

The Nazis used terror and opponents of the regime were persecuted. The Gestapo had wide powers and courts followed Nazi policy. However, this did not generally affect the popularity of Hitler's government because the accused were described as enemies of the German people and were often from weak minorities such as the Jews. Goebbels's propaganda was successful in hiding the worst aspects of the Nazis and exaggerating their successes. In particular, Hitler was portrayed as the great leader of all true Germans ✔.

Shows varied appeal of the Nazis.

Exam practice questions

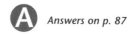

Answers on p. 87

(1) Compare the role and importance for the development of post-war Germany to 1965, of any **two** of the following: Konrad Adenauer; Ludwig Erhard; Walter Ulbricht.

[AQA question]

(2) **(a)** Analyse Hitler's aims in foreign policy to 1945.

(b) Assess Hitler's abilities as a war leader from 1939 to 1945.

Answers

(1)   **Key issue: The comparative roles of three German post-war leaders.**

Examiner's tip

Avoid narrative. Concentrate on comparisons.

Adenauer:
- Built up the Christian Democratic Party into a major force in West Germany (German Federal Republic). Chancellor 1949–1963. West Germany had long period of political stability. However, Adenauer was less effective in his later years.
- Helped to restore democracy to West Germany and gained the USA and Britain as allies. Reconciliation with France. Less enthusiastic about the Cold War than some other West Germans. Diplomatic links with the USSR.
- He was restrained when the Berlin Wall was built (1961). West Germany became partner in NATO and the European economy.

Erhard:
- Strength was the economy. Minister of Economic Affairs 1949–1963. Deputy Chancellor from 1957, the close partner of Adenauer. Succeeded Adenauer as Chancellor but lacked political and diplomatic skills. Relations with France became cooler. Fears of decline in the economy and his proposal to increase taxes was unpopular. Resigned in 1966.
- Encouraged the rebuilding of West German industry and the democratic organisation of trade unions, presiding over West Germany's 'economic miracle'. Took West Germany into western European economic organisations. In economic affairs, he can be seen as complementing the political skills of Adenauer.
- Adenauer and Erhard both won the trust of their allies and former enemies in the West. Depended on each other. Erhard was less successful as a politician and statesman than Adenauer.

Ulbricht:
- Leader of the Communists in post-war Germany; head of the Socialist Unity Party. Had full authority within (East) German Democratic Republic but was subservient to the USSR. Firm ally of Stalin. His power did not rely on democratic support but on Soviet patronage. GDR became an important part of the Soviet empire in eastern Europe, member of Comecon and the Warsaw Pact.
- Living standards rose. Some social reforms, although these did not compare with the achievements in the FDR. Although there were anti-government demonstrations (1953), stability was generally maintained. Berlin Wall halted the flight of refugees to the west.
- Like Adenauer and Erhard, he survived for a long time. Unlike them, his power ended only with his death. Created a state in East Germany and could claim credit for post-war recovery, but not equal to that in the West.

Answers

(2) (a)   Key issue: Analysis of Hitler's aims in foreign policy.

Examiner's tip

Focus on Hitler's aims. Avoid narrative. Note 1941 as the end point.

- Foreign policy was probably more important than domestic policy to Hitler. He planned the details personally. Strong foreign policies were necessary to display a country's power. Germany was reorganised to give priority to strengthening Germany's armed forces.
- Some historians argue that he continued previous policy of German expansion, others that he wanted revenge for Versailles, others that he had no clear aims but exploited opportunities as they arose, finally miscalculating over Poland.
- Nazi ideology was based on extreme nationalism and strong armies. Germans should be united in one country, by force if necessary. This involved the Anschluss with Austria and the occupation of the Sudetenland in Czechoslovakia.
- Living space (Lebensraum) was needed in the east; this involved Poland and Russia. Led to 1941 attack on Russia.
- Germany withdrew from the League of Nations (1933), began open rearmament (1935) and reoccupied the Rhineland (1936). The occupation of the Sudetenland, than all Czechoslovakia (1939), then the invasion of Poland.
- He was willing to compromise, e.g. Munich and the Nazi-Soviet Pact, but this was only another way of gaining his ultimate aims. Appeasement by Britain and France and Stalin's anxiety to agree to a Pact only encouraged Hitler.

(b)   Key issue: Assessment of Hitler's as a war leader.

Examiner's tip

Assessment involves examination of successes and failures. Avoid narrative of war.

- As Führer, Hitler had complete control of the military and the government. War was necessary and desirable to expand Germany's power. The armed services were increased in the 1930s with up-to-date-bombers and tanks (panzers).
- Hitler had no military training, a corporal in the First World War, but dictated overall planning (strategy) and often interfered in the details of fighting. Military commanders in the army, air force and navy were dismissed if they were unenthusiastic or suspected of disloyalty. Favoured large-scale schemes but was unrealistic about the demands on Germany.
- Blitzkrieg (lightning war) combined air power and land forces to overwhelm the enemy. Germany won swift victories against Poland (1939) in the east and Belgium, France, Holland, Denmark and Norway in the west (1940) then USSR (1941).
- Hitler made very serious mistakes. Declaration of war on the USA after Japan attacked Pearl Harbour was probably unnecessary and made an enemy of the most powerful country in the world. Underestimating the difficulty of invading Britain. Most serious mistake was the invasion of the USSR.
- He was inflexible and unwilling to take advice. The closing stages of the war particularly showed his ruthlessness and his lack of understanding of the real military position. Hitler's leadership led to the complete military defeat of Germany and the end of the Nazi Third Reich.

Mock exam

Answer one question   Time allowed: One hour

(1) (a) What were the factors which gave rise to Chartism?

(b) Why did Chartism fail?

[CCEA question]

(2) Source-based question: Disraeli's Second Ministry 1874–80

Michael Willis, an academic historian specialising in nineteenth-century history, Disraeli – Principles and Politics, *1989*.

When at last he gained power in 1874, he was able to successfully implement a series of social reforms to meet the physical needs of the urban poor which he had shown such concern about throughout his political life.

How valid is this interpretation of the social policies followed by Disraeli's Second Ministry, 1874–80?

[WJEC question]

(3) (a) Why was Ireland a continuing problem for British governments during the period 1909–1916?

(b) Assess the success of the Liberals from 1906 to 1914 in dealing with their domestic problems (excluding Ireland).

[OCR question]

(4) Why did the Labour Party win the 1945 general election?

(5) 'Through ceaseless activity and a triumph of will-power, she had by 1987 come as close to success as was possible for one self-sufficient human being.' How far do you agree with this assessment of Margaret Thatcher by Kenneth O. Morgan?

Mock exam

Answer one question   Time allowed: One hour

(1) How successful were the policies of Charles X?

[CCEA question]

(2) **(a)** Explain why Tsar Nicholas II agreed to the October Manifesto.

(b) 'The 1905 Revolution was successful in achieving political reform in Russia in the period up to 1914.' Explain why you agree or disagree with this view.

[AQA question]

(3) **(a)** Identify and explain the reasons why Mussolini came to power in Italy.

(b) Assess Mussolini's success by 1939 in making Italy a stable and prosperous country.

[OCR question]

(4) Compare the responsibility of Britain, France and Germany for the outbreak of the Second World War in 1939.

[OCR question]

(5) **(a)** Explain the major stages in western European co-operation from 1945 to the creation of the Single European Act in 1986.

(b) Analyse three reasons why most western European countries supported closer co-operation from 1945 to 1986.

Answers

(1)   **Key issue: Explanation and analysis of Chartism.**

Write an organised answer which presents causes in an order of priority. Avoid narrative of Chartism. Give examples of Chartist demands to link to causes.

(a)
- Chartists wanted more power for the industrial working classes who had not gained from the 1832 Reform Act. The People's Charter (1838) demanded more power for the working classes: universal manhood suffrage, annual parliaments, voting by ballot, equal electoral districts, payment of MPs and no property qualifications for MPs.
- Economic depression in the 1830s and 1840s caused much hardship. Factories reduced the independence of workers and destroyed many traditional skilled crafts. Social reforms in the 1830s, for example the new Poor Law, did not help the industrial working classes.
- Other groups failed to introduce important improvements, for example the London Working Men's Association, Birmingham Political Union and Owens's Grand National Consolidated Trade Union.

Write a brief plan to sort out your ideas. Put the causes in order of priority. Avoid narrative of the Chartists.

(b)
- Overall reasons: Support for the Chartists was weak, the opposition was strong. More interest in economic than in political issues. Violence discredited the movement.
- Leadership: Men such as Lovett, Attwood and O'Connor led the Chartists poorly. Never combined effectively. No national Chartist organisation and local organisations were inefficient.
- Differences about methods: Some wanted to use peaceful methods, or moral persuasion. Others favoured more extreme tactics, or physical force. Strikes and an armed uprising at Newport made people fear the outbreak of revolution.
- Few active Chartists: The movement never attracted the support of the prosperous middle classes or the better-paid members of the working classes. Little support for Chartism in the countryside. O'Connor's scheme for a Co-operative Land Settlement failed.
- Government tactics: The army suppressed most of the violence, although the government did not often use repressive methods. Leaders of the movement and ordinary Chartists often arrested. Governments supported by most MPs. Leading Whigs and Tories, such as Russell and Disraeli, opposed the movement.
- Economic reasons: General improvement in economic conditions after poor harvests in 1847–48. Anti-Corn Law League, demanding cheaper food and better led, was more attractive than the Chartists' political aims. Other members of the industrial working classes preferred to organise trade unions.

(2) **Key issue: Assessment of a quotation.**

Examiner's tip

Avoid a paraphrase of the source. Focus on the most important point – social policies – in the question.

- Willis's view: Willis's view is mostly justified, although there were limits to the government's achievements. Willis emphasises that Disraeli had long believed in social reform. His novels *Coninsgby* and *Sybil* and speeches claimed that Britain was divided into two nations.
- Tory democracy: Tory democracy was intended to introduce social reform and therefore to win support from the Liberals to the Conservative party. Reforms included public health, slum housing conditions, factory conditions, employment laws, education, the environment and safety at sea. Disraeli careful not to offend middle-class voters who paid most of the taxes. Many Conservatives, especially landowners who lived in the countryside, did not believe that governments should intervene in social affairs.
- Disraeli's role: Disraeli did not have detailed plans as Prime Minister. Encouraged other ministers but did not plan legislation himself. Cross, the Home Secretary, was particularly important in shaping new laws.
- Alternative views: Some historians argue that Disraeli was following the example of Gladstone and other Liberals and that his government was not very different from its predecessors.

(3) **Key issue: Analysis and assessment of pre-war Liberals.**

Examiner's tip

The key instruction in (a) is 'Why?'. Give reasons, not narrative. (b) should consider both success and failure.

(a) • Ireland had long been a problem for British governments. Failure of Home Rule Bills under Gladstone worsened the problem.
- Land ownership was a grievance because tenant farmers worked most land. Many owners lived in England.
- Sinn Fein was a more active and extreme nationalist movement. Involved in disorder in 1914 and the 1916 Easter Rising in Dublin. Also the Nationalist Volunteers and some syndicalists.
- Extreme Protestants in Ulster who were Unionists gained support in England. Carson, the leader of the Ulster Unionist movement, was an effective leader. Conservatives backed the Unionists, even calling for them to be armed.
- Doubts whether the Liberal government could rely on the army when the Curragh Mutiny took place.
- The 1914 war did not end the Irish problem. There were extremists on both sides who would not compromise.

(b) • Liberals' popularity was shown when they won three consecutive elections from 1906 to 1910.
- Trade Disputes Act (1906) and Trade Union Act (1913) ended some of the discrimination against trade unions but did not win support for the Liberals from the Labour Party.

- Pensions were introduced. National Insurance Act (1911) gave sickness benefits to many workers. In practice, the gains were limited.
- Attempts to reform the Poor Law failed and the unpopular workhouse system continued.
- Lloyd George proposals for a 'People's Budget' was successful in raising taxes to pay for the benefits and higher military expenditure. The House of Lords was forced to give in and its powers were reduced in the 1911 Parliament Act. Confirmed that the House of Commons was more important than the House of Lords.
- Government was unsuccessful in dealing with the Suffragettes. Opposed bills to introduce women's suffrage and the Suffragettes became more violent. By 1914 some Liberal leaders were willing to concede but the 1914 war made the issue less important.

(4)   **Key issue: Analysis of 1945 election result.**

Examiner's tip

Consider both long- and short-term reasons. Explain Labour's advantages and the Conservative disadvantages.

- The 1945 general election was a massive victory for the Labour Party. Majority of almost 150. Labour Party won the support of most of the electorate and from much wider social groups in towns and the countryside than before. People wanted a better Britain after the war, with social reforms, full employment, good houses and a national health service.
- Attlee, the leader, was quiet, but a skilful and effective politician; Churchill's respected deputy during the Second World War. Other Labour leaders were popular because of their work and talents: Bevan, a former trade union leader and Minister of Labour during the war, Morrison, who had led the London County Council, and wartime Minister of Supply, Bevin was a powerful speaker and thinker.
- The Labour Party was not responsible for the hardships of the 1930s or the outbreak of the Second World War. Conservatives were blamed for the 1930s and were believed to oppose social and economic reform. A Conservative government had been too weak to stop Hitler and prevent the Second World War.
- Churchill had a high reputation as the man who won the war. He was also distrusted by some as a warmonger. Attempts by the Conservatives to portray the Labour Party as unpatriotic backfired.
- The Conservatives fought the election mostly as a vote of confidence in Churchill's wartime leadership and did not offer the policies for which people were looking. Not given credit for some of the planning which had taken place during the war, for example Butler's Education Act, plans for a new national insurance scheme.
- The Labour victory was part of a swing in western Europe towards left-wing socialist parties after the war.

(5)   **Key issue: Assessment of a judgement on Thatcher as Prime Minister.**

Examiner's tip

Highlight the most important parts of Morgan's claims. Show where you agree and disagree.

- 'Ceaseless activity and a triumph of will-power': An achievement was to gain power as the first female Prime Minister in Britain. However, she did little to promote other women in Parliament and her Cabinet. Dominated the Conservative Party and more effective than opposition leaders. Her policies were sometimes unpopular with some in Cabinet. She replaced moderate Conservatives with right-wing ministers but her later years saw splits. Heseltine, Minister of Defence, and Howe, Deputy Prime Minister, resigned.

- 'As close to success as was possible for one self-sufficient human being' by 1987. She won 3 elections (1979, 1983, 1987). By 1988, the longest-serving British Prime Minister in twentieth century. Quotation is valid but 1988–1990 saw failure.

- Very wide personal appeal, although she was controversial and much disliked by some.

- Introduced new economic ideas, monetarism, against state subsidies. Initial success but problems later. Unemployment increased to more than three million. Old industries disappeared. Poll tax very unpopular.

- Attitude to Europe was uncertain. Agreed to single market but also very critical of European Community. On bad terms with many European leaders but a firm ally of American President Reagan. Victory in Falklands War (1982) increased popularity and helped to win 1983 election.

- Unpopularity in opinion polls and splits in party, especially over Europe, led to her resignation after she narrowly defeated leadership challenge by Heseltine (1990). The Iron Lady dominated British politics for 10 years and changed ideas and policies considerably.

Answers

(1)   **Key issue: Assessment of Charles X.**

Examiner's tip

Explain the different groups opposed to Charles X. Discuss the particular causes of the 1830 Revolution. Consider some of Charles X's achievements.

- The aims of Charles X: He wished to restore the ancien régime and destroy the changes in France since the 1789 Revolution. As the Comte D'Artois, he was the leader of the Ultras (extreme royalists) during the reign of Louis XVIII. He opposed the Charter, issued by Louis XVIII, which limited some of the powers of the King.
- Early opposition after his accession in 1824: His coronation alarmed many because the ceremony resembled those of the ancien régime. The Bourbon flag replaced the revolutionary tricolour.
- The émigrés: An indemnity was paid to the émigrés. Angered the middle classes (bourgeoisie) because it was paid for by their taxes.
- Religion: Control of education given to the Church. Bishop became minister of education. Jesuits were readmitted to France and sacrilege was made punishable by death. Offended anti-clerical people.
- Ministers: Villele dismissed because of growing unrest. Replaced by moderate Martignac. Change in policy was temporary. Polignac, an extreme royalist and former émigré, replaced Martignac. Clashed with the Chamber of Deputies, which insisted that ministers should pursue more popular policies.
- Positive achievements: Successes of the reign did not compensate for the failures. Algeria was conquered and helped to establish a French empire in Africa.
- Middle classes led 1830 Revolution. Working classes of the cities, especially Paris, disliked Charles X's policies because of worsening economic conditions. He was blamed for growing poverty. Given no credit for some of the improvements in industry and transport. The Ordinances of St. Cloud would have abolished the Charter. Hostile crowds gathered in Paris to prevent the King seizing power in a coup d'état. Charles X lost control of the army.

(2)   **Key issue: Examination of Russia 1905–14.**

Examiner's tip

This is a narrow question. Long-term causes must be linked closely to 1905.

(a) • The 1905 Revolution seemed a serious challenge to Nicholas II's tsarist government. Climax of much unrest by peasants, industrial workers (proletariat) and students. Defeat by Japan caused anger in Russia.
- Widespread risings and strikes, especially in Moscow, Odessa and St. Petersburg in 1905. Committees of workers (soviets) were set up. The battleship *Potemkin* mutinied.
- Loyal army was used to suppress a march led by Father Gapon and the other risings. Witte persuaded the Tsar to issue the October Manifesto to win over the opposition. The Manifesto promised a Duma (national assembly), elected on a broad franchise, as a concession to those who called for reforms.

(b) • Agree with the quotation: The October Manifesto won over some radicals, for example Octobrists. Kadets agreed to take part in elections. The Duma was the first example in Russia of an elected, national institution.

• Extreme groups such as the Bolsheviks were weakened. Leaders, including Lenin, and many supporters were exiled, imprisoned or went into exile.

• Disagree with the quotation: Fundamental Laws (1906) reversed some of the concessions of the October Manifesto. Tsar had supreme autocratic power and could issue emergency legislation. Four Duma met from 1906 to 1916 but none was effective. Nicholas II was unwilling to allow them significant powers. Members disagreed on their demands.

• Russia in 1914: Russia seemed stable. Nicholas II was respected. The army and police kept opposition under control. The economy was growing with increased foreign investments. Social reforms, including insurance and education, helped to maintain political stability.

(3)   **Key issue: Explanation and analysis of Mussolini's rule.**

(a) • Government and economic weakness: Constitutional monarchy was weak. Governments were unstable and changed frequently. Italy had few natural resources and little industry. Difficult to recover from the effects of the First World War.

• Post-war disillusion: Italy had been a member of the Triple Alliance but changed to the victorious Triple Entente. Italy given limited gains in the peace settlements. Italians believed that they had been promised more if they changed sides.

• Appeal of Fascism: Mussolini's fascists promised to bring order to a corrupt political system. Mussolini aimed to restore Italy's military power and gain more territories. Fascists appealed to the middle classes, industrialists and many youth. Mussolini had an exaggerated reputation as a war hero. Edited a newspaper (*Il Popolo d'Italia*) to spread his ideas. A charismatic orator and a forceful leader who was willing to take bold measures to gain power (The March on Rome). Fears that the communists would seize power.

• Establishment of power: King invited Mussolini to form a government (1924). Given dictatorial power for one year. Used this time to introduce a law which allowed fascists to claim most of the seats in the chamber. Opponents were suppressed; Matteotti, the socialist leader, was murdered.

This is a two-part question: 'stable and prosperous'. Both should be given equal attention.

(b) • Stability: Opposition groups were suppressed. Italy was a one-party state. The fascists nominated candidates for elections. Controlled the police. Lateran treaties (1929) ended the quarrel between the Roman Catholic Church and the Italian State. Fascists organised social, recreational and leisure activities for the workers. Italy had few positive gains in foreign policy by 1939 but Mussolini was admired for playing a major role in European affairs.

• Opposition continued outside the political system. Mussolini's government was not as ruthless as those of Hitler and Stalin.

• Prosperity: Strikes were outlawed. Industrial disputes were settled by the National Council of Corporations, controlled by the fascists. Mussolini encouraged many public works. Many of Mussolini's economic achievements were exaggerated by propaganda. Output figures were inflated. Grain was less suitable than other crops in many parts of Italy. A high exchange rate for the lira hindered exports. The standard of living remained low.

(4) **Key issue: Comparison of responsibility for the Second World War.**

Put the countries in your order of priority. Concentrate on analysis, not narrative.

Germany's role:
• Responsible for the immediate cause of war because of the invasion of Poland. Followed previous take-overs of Austria and Czechoslovakia. Hitler broke promises, for example Munich, and ruthlessly bullied small countries. Hitler agreed alliances with Mussolini and Stalin. Probably knew that the attack on Poland might result in war with Britain and France.

• Hitler rearmed Germany and took control of the army. Domestic economy aimed to make Germany self-sufficient in case war broke out.

• Historians disagree whether he deliberately started a general war in 1939. Some think that Germany was not ready for war, others that military expansion was necessary to achieve 'lebensraum'. Some argue that he gambled that Britain and France would back down over Poland as at Munich.

Britain's role:
• Appeasement was popular in Britain; opponents of appeasement were few. Some thought that Germany had genuine grievances about the Versailles settlement, others that the British economy and military forces were too weak to fight a war. Nazis might be useful in the struggle with communism. Hitler was admired for restoring order to Germany.

• Chamberlain was convinced that he could deal with Hitler. Diplomacy could work if Hitler was allowed reasonable concessions. Anschluss with Austria and the take-over of Czechoslovakia were not of vital importance to Britain and the guarantees to Poland and other countries were not emphasised until too late.

France's role:

- For different reasons, French politicians and the public opposed war with Germany. French army and economy had not recovered from the effects of the First World War. Most feared German military strength; some right-wing parties sympathised with Hitler.
- France backed down when Hitler reoccupied the Rhineland. Gave guarantees to defend central European countries which it could not fulfil. France usually followed Britain's policy. Played a minor role over Austria and Czechoslovakia and Hitler did not believe that France was a serious threat.

(5) (a)   Key issue: Explanation of stages in western European co-operation.

Examiner's tip

Discuss political, economic and military issues. Explain why developments were important.

- Political stages: Council of Europe (1949) encouraged co-operation about human rights and freedom. All western European countries were members by 1986, including Switzerland. Cyprus and Malta also members. Led to European Parliament. Single European Act (1986) accepted by 12 countries in European Community. Increased powers of European Parliament. More common decision-making. Important because most countries were willing to surrender some individual powers. End of idea of complete nation state.
- Economic stages: European Coal and Steel Community (1950s) resulted from Schumann Plan. Planned heavy industries and policy to oil, nuclear and hydroelectric power. Important as the first major step to economic co-operation.
- Common Market or European Economic Community (EEC) set up by Treaty of Rome (1957). Abolition of internal tariffs, free movement of workers and goods. Originally 6 members, led by France and West Germany. Britain joined Common Market 1973. More powerful than alternative European Free Trade Association. By 1986, EFTA worked closely with EEC. Important because individual countries gave up some control of their economies to ensure greater prosperity.
- Military stages: Brussels Treaty (1948) a military and diplomatic alliance. North Atlantic Treaty Organisation (NATO), set up (1949), included western European countries, Britain and USA. West Germany (1955). Result of Cold War, to defend west Europe against USSR. Led by USA. France withdrew (1966), wanting more independence from USA. Proposal for European Defence Community (1952) of major Continental countries, not Britain. Failed because of French opposition. Important in helping to restore European military power after the Second World War as a major force in the Cold War.
- Also: European Court of Justice, European Investment Bank to aid underdeveloped countries, Euratom to harmonise peaceful nuclear policy. Important to show the range of European co-operation.

(b)   Key issue: Analysis of reasons for western European co-operation.

Examiner's tip

Select three different reasons. Analytical answers get higher marks than narrative.

- The co-operation between France and West Germany, enemies since 1870, was crucial in political and economic developments. Less important in military developments because de Gaulle's France had more independent policies. Also helped to bring peace between Germany, Italy and other countries in western Europe.
- Economic damage of the Second World War needed co-operation to bring prosperity. Economic nationalism less important as economies improved. Most countries in western Europe joined the Common Market by 1986; others wished to.
- The Cold War persuaded western European countries that alliances (e.g. NATO) were necessary for defence against USSR and its allies. Also involved USA. Apart from France, NATO remained the centre of European defence. Britain also pursued an independent military policy at times, e.g. retaining its nuclear weapons.

Mock exam

Answer two questions
Time allowed: One hour 30 minutes

(1) 'Tory Democracy was a fraud probably, but a fraud nonetheless.' (Lord Rosebery) Consider the arguments for and against this Liberal view of Disraeli as a party leader and Prime Minister between 1867 and 1880.

[OCR question]

(2) Assess the success of the welfare state in solving the problems of poverty since 1945.

(3) Consider the arguments for and against the claim that war has been the major cause of social and political change in twentieth-century Britain.

(4) Why was Ireland partitioned in 1922?

(5) How far do you agree that the Labour government of 1945–50 was the most revolutionary of the twentieth century?

Mock exam

Answer two questions
Time allowed: One hour 30 minutes

(1) Which tsar from 1801 to 1914 was most successful in achieving his aims?

(2) To what extent did Khrushchev dismantle the Stalinist political and economic structure during his time in power in the USSR?

[AQA question]

(3) Why did liberalism remain weak in Germany from 1815 to 1919?

(4) 'Fascism, unlike communism, lacked a coherent ideology.' How justified is this view?

(5) How dangerous was the Cold War to peace in Europe from 1945 to the reunification of Germany in 1990?

Answers

(1)   Key issue: Evaluation of an historical judgement.

Examiner's tips

Define Tory Democracy. Balance the argument between 'for' and 'against' but make clear which is more justified.

- Lord Rosebery was Liberal Prime Minister (1894–95). This affects the judgement of his assessment. More interested in foreign and imperial policy than domestic affairs, especially reform. His view was not that of a typical Liberal.
- Disraeli gave a new direction to Conservative policies on electoral and social reforms. Supported 'One Nation', which later became known as Tory Democracy. Tried to link different social classes, with the rich helping the poor. There should be an alliance between the monarchy, upper, middle and lower classes to benefit all. Tory Democracy included support for the 1867 Reform Act and social reforms, including changes in education, factory reform, public health, housing and shipping laws.
- Disraeli was an effective party leader, uniting a party that had been divided since Peel's fall in 1846. Policies and more democratic organisation of the party won support from the working and especially the middle class – important in winning elections. Disraeli's ministers combined traditional aristocratic ministers, for example Salisbury and men from different social backgrounds. Cross: banker and solicitor, Hardy: iron manufacturer, WH Smith: news agencies. Gorst built up the party organisation. Cross was responsible for much social legislation.
- Disraeli was more concerned about imperial affairs, which he saw as helping British interests. Bought the Suez Canal shares to safeguard the route to India. Queen Victoria became Empress of India in 1876. Helped to make imperialism more popular in Britain.
- Criticism of the social reforms: they usually relied on local authorities taking action and raising money to finance schemes. Disraeli relied on support from the middle classes. Increasing taxes to pay would be unpopular.
- Most measures became law early in Disraeli's ministry. Little done after 1876, although this was partly because of wars in Africa and disruptive tactics by Parnell's Irish Nationalist MPs. Extent of Tory Democracy compared well with Gladstone's policies but not the beginning of a welfare state. Did not prevent the growth of socialism. Its success was limited but it was not, as Rosebery claimed, a fraud.

(2)   Key issue: Assessment of the welfare state.

Examiner's tip

This is a synoptic question. You should try to link a range of factors.

- Welfare state, protecting the weakest 'from the cradle to the grave', was developed from the early twentieth century but was fully established after 1945. Part of the transformation of Britain by the post-war Labour government but was continued by Conservative governments.
- Included National Health Service and National Insurance Act, subsidised housing, better educational opportunities and child allowances aimed to combat poverty.
- National income doubled from 1945 to 1980: an age of general affluence. Most people's standard of living increased, with more private houses, cars and domestic equipment. Leisure activities boomed.

- Costs of the welfare state were unexpectedly high and expenditure had to be cut back by successive governments.
- Changing economic and social patterns contributed to the poverty of the lower classes. The economic pattern of 'boom and bust' since 1945 prevented a steady attack on poverty. Rising unemployment from the 1970s caused more poverty. The increase in divorce and single-parent families affected a larger proportion of the population. Overall, the gap between rich and poor (relative poverty) grew. Particular groups affected by poverty included immigrants and people from racial minorities.

(3)   **Key issue: Comparison of different arguments about social change.**

Examiner's tip

Avoid narrative. Deal first with war, then other factors. A synoptic approach, with a wide range of points, is better than an analysis of particular developments.

- Twentieth-century wars were different in nature from earlier wars. Armies became larger after conscription. Methods of warfare were more destructive. Effects of war on the civilian population were greater because of damage to property, food shortages. Every family was involved.
- War encouraged the demand for more democracy and better living conditions. Made governments more powerful. Conscription was introduced. Emergency laws limited people's freedoms. The population became more used to government intervention than in the nineteenth century.
- Changing balance of political parties was important. Conservatives were influential throughout the century but had to adapt their policies to reflect the changing electorate. Labour Party replaced the Liberals as their challengers and extended their social reforms after the Second World War. Post-1945 Conservative governments mostly followed similar social policies.
- During the 1930s and from 1945 to about 1960, memories of war were key factor but after 1960 other issues became more important. Patterns of employment changed with decline of manufacturing and heavy industry and increase in light industry and the service trades. This affected the prosperity of particular regions and groups of the population. Overall, there was more affluence.
- Decline of the empire was accompanied by changing attitudes to Europe in most people although attitudes to political co-operation were divided. Women had more opportunities for employment and independence. Youth culture was a new phenomenon.
- The Thatcher era reflected a distrust of planning and an admiration of individualism, contrary to opinion after the two world wars. The certainty of Britain's position in the world in 1918 and its apparently leading role was a contrast to the uncertainties of 2000.

(4)   **Key issue: Analysis of reasons for the partition of Ireland.**

Examiner's tip

The question asks 'Why' and you should write reasons, not narrative. Avoid too much background.

- Attempts in the nineteenth and early twentieth century to solve the Irish problem had failed. Religious and land issues had been largely solved but independence was the most important issue.
- 1916 Easter Rising hardened attitudes on both sides. Proclamation of the Dail and the Republic became effective in some parts of Ireland. After the war, the British government lost authority in spite of the Black and Tans and Auxiliary Division. Army advised that order could be restored only by a full-scale war.
- British Liberal politicians accepted independence reluctantly, not out of principle. Some Conservatives agreed but many supported the Unionists. Labour Party supported independence. Pressure on the Irish nationalists to agree. De Valera, president of the Dail, was willing to negotiate. Some members of the IRA refused to accept a divided Ireland but were outmanoeuvred by the politicians and moderates.
- Disagreement about the terms of independence. British politicians pressed for dominion status to keep Ireland within the Empire. This was agreed. Britain also retained ports within the Irish Republic for the navy. What should happen to Ulster? Lloyd George proposed a small Ulster that might in future have to join an independent Ireland. This satisfied the Conservatives and Ulster MPs strengthened them at Westminster.

(5)   **Key issue: Assessment of the significance of twentieth-century governments.**

Examiner's tip

This is a synoptic question. You must show a wide knowledge but do not try to mention every government.

- 'Most revolutionary' involves changes in different areas: political, economic and social. Few governments tried to introduce major changes. Most sought minor changes or only survival. No government was as revolutionary as some in Continental Europe, e.g. Lenin's Russia, Mussolini's Italy, Hitler's Germany. 'Revolutionary' must be understood in British history.
- Liberal government (1905–15 but First World War broke out 1914). Campbell-Bannerman, then Asquith, led governments that carried out major reforms. 'People's Budget' introduced old-age pensions. Laid foundations of welfare state. Parliament Act removed most powers of House of Lords. 'A triumph of Democracy' (Scaife) that confirmed the supremacy of an elected House of Commons. Political and social reforms but not important economic changes. The most influential government in the early twentieth century.
- Labour government (1945–50). Attlee's ministry carried out radical economic changes, nationalisation of major industries. National Health Service. Education reforms. Decolonisation began; independence of India and Pakistan a major step, Empire became Commonwealth. Political, economic, social and diplomatic changes. The most influential government in the mid-twentieth century.

- Conservative governments (1979–1990). Thatcher's ministries introduced new economic and financial ideas. Nationalised industries privatised, e.g. gas, electricity, water. More people bought shares. More private and fewer council houses. Three election victories changed political pattern. Ended post-war period of similar governments avoiding extreme left- or right-wing policies (government by consensus). Challenged assumptions about the economic importance of the State. Social changes, with more shareholders and reliance on private enterprise. The most influential government in the late twentieth century.
- Overall, Labour government extended the Liberal reforms and 1945–50 was more important than 1905–14. But Conservative governments changed direction. Most revolutionary because of extent and speed of changes.

Answers

(1) **Key issue: Comparison of Russian tsars.**

Examiner's tip

A synoptic question that requires understanding of an extended period. Put your arguments in order of your priority.

Alexander I (1801–25):

- Russia took a leading role in the defeat of Napoleon and was important in post-war diplomacy. But other European countries distrusted Russia. The Holy Alliance was a failure.
- Alexander changed between repression and liberalism at home. A Council of State was created and some local assemblies established. Finland and Poland were given some self-government. Later policies were more conservative. The reign ended with the Decembrist Revolt.

Nicholas I (1825–55):

- Policies of 'Autocracy, Orthodoxy and Nationalism' were adopted. Nicholas was mostly a reactionary, completing the suppression of the Decembrists. The secret police (Third Section) dealt harshly with liberals. Education was controlled. However, some signs of reform. State serfs were given personal freedom and he considered more emancipation. Laws were codified.
- Polish Revolt (1830) was defeated and Russia intervened with Austria to suppress rebellion in Hungary (1849). Nicholas II failed in his aim to expand at the expense of Turkey and Russia faced defeat in the Crimean War at his death.

Alexander II (1855–81):

- Aim was to preserve autocracy by changing inefficient institutions. Reforms to serfdom, education, justice and the military but they encouraged rather than deterred unrest. Poland rebelled. Violent groups (People's Will, anarchists, nihilists) threatened revolution. Attempts to assassinate the Tsar finally succeeded. Economy generally improved, especially railways, but Russia still lagged behind western European countries.
- Alexander regained some of the losses in the Crimean War, adopting a policy of Panslavism. Some success in a war against Turkey and Russia advanced in central Asia and Afghanistan.

Alexander III (1881–94):

- Aim was complete autocracy. No concessions to liberals. Minority national groups, including Jews, were persecuted. Opposition parties, for example Marxists, were prosecuted strongly. With Pobedonostsev, Alexander III preferred Russification to westernisation. Alexander III achieved his aims in domestic affairs but they caused problems in the future.
- Foreign policy changed from friendship with Bismarck's Germany to a French alliance when Bismarck, then William II, chose Austria as an ally. Russian advance to the east continued.

Nicholas II (1894–1917 but note that question ends in 1914):

- Nicholas II continued the autocratic aims of Alexander III. 1905 Revolution revealed opposition but order was restored. October Manifesto promised some reform but there was little change. Dumas were mostly ineffective because of lack of support from the tsar and his ministers.
- Economy improved with investments from Britain and France. Railway system expanded. Stolypin's agricultural policies encouraged the kulaks and there were some social reforms. However, there were industrial strikes and rural riots. Russia's military and naval weakness was apparent in the war against Japan and Nicholas's aims of strengthening the army by 1914 had not been achieved.
- Regime was mostly successful to 1914 in suppressing opposition. Bolshevik leaders were in prison or exile and the regime appeared to be reasonably stable.

(2)   **Key issue: Assessment of Khrushchev's policies.**

Examiner's tip

Questions asking 'How far?' require you to explain extents and limits of policies.

- Khrushchev (Party Secretary) came to power after a period of uncertainty after Stalin's death. Overcame important rivals for power, for example Malenkov, Beria immediately after the death of Stalin, Marshal Zhukov and Molotov. Took three years to gain the leadership, which was never as unchallenged as Stalin's.
- Lacked the personal pre-eminence of Stalin. 'Collective leadership' recognised the limits of his power as well as a reaction against Stalinism. Initially shared power with Bulganin as Prime Minister until 1958.
- Twentieth Party Congress (1956): Khrushchev attacked 'the cult of personality' and attacked the excesses of Stalin's regime. Aim was to preserve communism but to modify the system. Some easing of political persecution but the gulag system continued and the changes had fewer, rather than more, effects on the police system. Strict policies to the arts were modified but media were still strictly controlled.
- Economic policy revised. Sixth Five-Year Plan (1956–60) emphasised heavy industry. The Sputnik (1957) seemed to indicate the supremacy of Soviet technology under Khrushchev but this was later seen as misleading. Changes in agriculture were attempted. Farming of virgin land was encouraged but unsuitable regions, technological inefficiency and inflexible communist organisation prevented its success.
- Khrushchev weakened within the USSR by instability in eastern Europe, for example Czechoslovakia, east Berlin, Poland, Hungary. Khrushchev announced 'different roads to socialism', which contrasted with Stalin's policy of centralisation. Opened divisions about future policy within the USSR.
- Khrushchev's fall (1964) resulted from his insecure hold on power and continued opposition to policies of destalinisation. Kosygin and especially Brezhnev were more conservative. Showed that Khrushchev's changes were slight and temporary. However, there was an end to terror. Khrushchev, Malenkov and Bulganin were not purged as under Stalin but died peacefully.

(3)   Key issue: Analysis of German liberalism.

Examiner's tip

This is a synoptic question that needs discussion of the extended period from 1815 to 1919.

- Liberalism was weak in 1815: associated with nationalism and the French Revolution. Vienna settlement created a German Confederation of 39 states without a central administration. Controlled by conservative Austria. Metternich persuaded King of Prussia not to grant a liberal constitution.
- Carlsbad Decrees (1819) prevented political meetings, ensured strict censorship and controlled the educational system. Few opportunities for Liberals to express their ideas peacefully. Frankfurt Parliament (1848) seemed a Liberal triumph. Elected by a wide suffrage. Most of its members were middle class, including lawyers and university teachers. It failed to agree a political programme and lacked military strength. Frederick William of Prussia refused to co-operate. Most members withdrew and the Parliament was easily suppressed by military force.
- Bismarck was anti-Liberal. He came to power in 1862 when he defeated the Liberals' attempts to block the military budget. Parliamentary consent became less important than 'blood and iron'. Liberals supported a united Germany in 1870 but it had been achieved without their help.
- Constitution of the new German Empire was apparently democratic. Elected Reichstag and a large franchise. In reality, it was authoritarian and illiberal. The Kaiser appointed the Chancellor and other ministers. Prussia had the majority of votes in the Bundesrat, which was more important than the Reichstag. From 1871 to 1890, Bismarck supported or opposed the Liberals depending on his other problems. They were useful allies against the Catholic Church and socialists but were discarded when he adopted protectionism after 1880.
- William II's rule favoured the conservative junkers and officer class. His foreign policies were popular as he advanced Germany's claims to greatness. Liberal warnings about the danger of war were ineffective. Outbreak of war in 1914 led to considerable support for the authoritarian Kaiser.
- Defeat in the war resulted in the liberal Weimar Republic: republican, with proportional representation and guaranteed rights. Liberals were not popular because of the circumstances behind the establishment of the Weimar Republic. Accused of sabotaging the war effort.

(4) Key issue: Discussion of two political theories.

Examiner's tip

Avoid vagueness. Support your general argument with examples.

Fascism:
- Hitler, like Mussolini, claimed that fascism was based on a clear philosophy. He later claimed that *Mein Kampf* was both important and unimportant. It probably reflected his basic ideas accurately. Mussolini paid less importance to theories but did write about *The Doctrine of Fascism* and supported the *Enciclopedia Italiana* that included fascist ideas. Origins of fascism were the experience of the First World War, ineffective democracy and economic hardship rather than the theories of writers such as Nietzsche.

- Fascism claimed to be an alternative to right- and left-wing politics to unite all groups in a shared nation. In practice, in Germany and Italy, the fascists pursued right-wing policies that limited power to a few. Fascism promised real liberty but individual liberty was unimportant.
- Hitler believed that racial purity was an important aspect of fascism. Non-Aryans were not fully human. Race was less important to Italian fascism. Anti-liberal and anti-communist. Fascism claimed to be 'socialist' to benefit all citizens. Large state economic enterprises but also private enterprise for the rich. Workers' rights disappeared.

Communism:

- Marx's ideas (*Das Kapital*, *The Communist Manifesto*) were influential from the late nineteenth century. Included political and economic analysis. Supported revolution against the existing social order. Proletariat would overcome the bourgeoisie, leading to a classless society. Bolsheviks, extreme Marxists in Russia, supported revolution as a necessary and inevitable development.
- Lenin implemented communist policies of state control and the monopoly of the communist party. New Economic Policy (NEP) adopted because of shortages but did not basically change the communist system. Stalin less interested in ideas. Enforced some general principles such as the domination of the party and state economic control but also repression of workers that contradicted the ideals of Marx.
- Defeat of Germany and Italy in the Second World War discredited fascism. Victory justified communism to the USSR and eastern Europe. Alternative to American capitalism to minority in western Europe.

(5)   **Key issue: Assessment of the danger of the Cold War.**

Examiner's tip

Avoid causes of the Cold War. Focus on danger to peace in Europe.

- Tensions in Europe at the end of Second World War; disagreement about influence of USSR and western governments. Europe important to USSR and USA. Problem of reconstruction and treatment of Germany a core problem.
- Soviet takeover of Czechoslovakia by 1948 and control of other eastern European powers alarmed western Europe. Division of Germany into Federal Republic and Democratic Republic increased tensions. Berlin blockade (1948–49) endangered peace. Military, political and economic threat.
- North Atlantic Treaty Organisation (1949) followed by Warsaw Pact (1955). Two rival military alliances faced each other, led by USA and USSR.
- Unrest in eastern Europe increased intensity of Cold War, e.g. Hungary and Poland (1956), building of Berlin Wall (1961), Czechoslovakia (1968). West decided intervention would result in open warfare.
- Attempts to modify Cold War began in 1950s. Geneva Conference (1955), Rapacki Plan (1957). Brandt, Federal German Chancellor, had policy of Ostpolitik to improve relations with Democratic Republic and other eastern European countries. Honecker, GDR leader, was more moderate. Both Germanys signed treaty of friendship (1972). Final stage was reunification of Germany (1990). Marked end of Cold War in Europe.

For your notes

For your notes

For your notes